Euro cottage
Plain Yogurt
Limon
mid.
Turmeric

COOKING
FROM ABOVE
ASIAN

COOKING FROM ABOVE

ASIAN

JODY VASSALLO

PHOTOGRAPHY BY CLIVE BOZZARD-HILL

✳ ✳ ✳

hamlyn

First published in France in 2007 under the title
Les basiques d'Asie, by Hachette Livre (Marabout)
Copyright © 2007 Hachette Livre (Marabout)

© Text Jody Vassallo
Photography by Clive Bozzard-Hill
Styling by Sonia Lucano

An Hachette UK Company
www.hachette.co.uk

First published in Great Britain in 2009 by
Hamlyn, a division of Octopus Publishing Group Ltd
2–4 Heron Quays, London E14 4JP
www.octopusbooksusa.com

Copyright © English edition
Octopus Publishing Group Ltd 2009

Distributed in the United States and Canada by
Hachette Book Group
237 Park Avenue, New York, NY 10017 USA

ISBN 978-0-600-61997-0

Printed and bound in Singapore

10 9 8 7 6 5 4 3 2 1

Measurements Standard level spoon measurements
are used in all recipes.

Nuts This book includes dishes made with nuts and
nut derivatives. It is advisable for those with known
allergic reactions to nuts and nut derivatives and
those who may be potentially vulnerable to these
allergies, such as pregnant and nursing mothers,
invalids, the elderly, babies, and children, to avoid
dishes made with nuts and nut oils. It is also advisable
to check the labels of preprepared ingredients for
the possible inclusion of nut derivatives.

Eggs should be large unless otherwise stated. The
Department of Health advises that eggs should not
be consumed raw. This book contains dishes made
with raw or lightly cooked eggs. It is advisable for
more vulnerable people, such as pregnant and nursing
mothers, invalids, the elderly, babies, and young
children, to avoid uncooked or lightly cooked dishes
made with eggs. Once prepared these dishes should
be kept refrigerated and used promptly.

Milk should be full fat unless otherwise stated.

Butter is unsalted unless otherwise stated.

Fresh herbs should be used unless otherwise stated.
If unavailable use dried herbs as an alternative but
halve the quantities stated.

Ovens should be preheated to the specific
temperature—if using a fan-assisted oven, follow
manufacturer's instructions for adjusting the time
and the temperature.

INTRODUCTION

When I think of quick and easy delicious meals I'm immediately drawn to Asian cuisine. Most recipes only call for a wok or pan, and if you have a rice cooker then you just need to push a button to cook your rice. Some of the ingredients can, I know, be a little tricky to locate, but these days more and more stores are stocking a wide range of Asian ingredients.

The most important thing to remember about cooking the recipes in this book is to get everything chopped and ready before you turn on the heat; this is because many stir-fries take less than 10 minutes to cook.

So pick a cuisine—Thai, Japanese, Vietnamese, Chinese, or Indonesian—and select a recipe, follow the step-by-step photographs and see for yourself just how easy the dishes from these countries are to prepare. Before you know it you will have a repertoire that will rival your local take-out.

CONTENTS

SEASONING A WOK

❧ **PREPARATION: 5 MINUTES • COOKING: 20 MINUTES** ❧

NOTE: Each time you use the wok, make sure you wash it only in hot water—do not use soap. Dry over a high heat and brush lightly with oil.

1	Wash the brand new wok in soapy water, scrubbing away any machine oil. Rinse under cold running water and dry.	2	Brush the entire surface with peanut oil.
3	Put the wok over a high heat and heat until blackened. Let cool.	4	Mop up the excess oil with paper towels. Repeat the brushing, blackening, cooling, and mopping about 3 times until the wok darkens.

HOW TO COOK RICE

⇒ MAKES 4 CUPS • PREPARATION: 5 MINUTES • COOKING: 15 MINUTES ⇐

1⅓ cups jasmine or white rice

1 2
3 4

1	Rinse the rice under cold running water until the water runs clear.	2	Put the rice in a large pan, cover with cold water, and bring to a boil.
3	Cook until tunnels form in the rice. Reduce the heat to low and cover the rice.	4	Let stand until all the liquid has been absorbed. Gently separate the grains with a fork.

SEASONED SUSHI RICE

❋ **MAKES 4** CUPS • PREPARATION: 5 MINUTES + 1 HOUR DRAINING • COOKING: 20 MINUTES ❋

1½ cups sushi rice
1½ cups water

DRESSING:
2 tablespoons rice vinegar
1 tablespoon superfine sugar
2 teaspoons salt

1 2
3 4

1	Wash the rice then drain for 1 hour. Put the rice in a pan, add the measured water, and bring to a boil. Boil for 5 minutes.	2	Take off the heat. Cover and cook (or stand) for 10 minutes until the liquid has been absorbed.
3	Heat all the dressing ingredients in a pan until the sugar has dissolved. Spread the rice out on a large tray, pour over the dressing and mix in.	4	Cover with a damp kitchen towel and let cool completely. Use in sushi rolls, chirashi sushi, and temaki sushi. Sushi rice only keeps for 1 day.

STARTERS

SOUPS

SNACKS

APPETIZERS

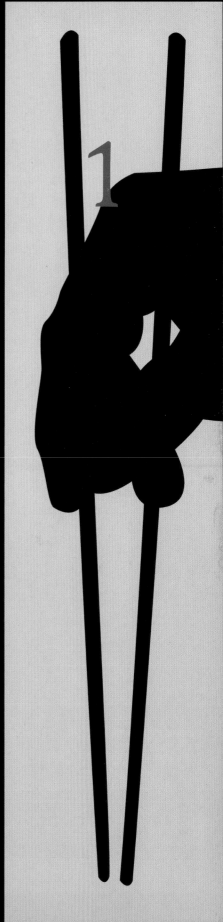

1

TOM YUM GOONG

❧ **SERVES 4 • PREPARATION: 20 MINUTES • COOKING: 15 MINUTES** ❧

8 large raw shrimp
4 garlic cloves, crushed
3 lemongrass stalks, sliced

7 oz white mushrooms, halved
2 ripe tomatoes, cut into wedges
3 small red chiles, halved

5 kaffir lime leaves
3 tablespoons fish sauce
2 tablespoons lime juice, to serve

1

2

3

4

5

6

1	Peel and devein the shrimp, setting aside the shells.	2	Put the shells in a pan with 3 cups water and bring to a boil.	3	When the shells are pink, strain off the bouillon and discard the shells.
4	Add the remaining ingredients, bring to a boil, then simmer for 5 minutes.	5	Add the shrimp and cook for 3 minutes. Remove from the heat.	6	Stir in the lime juice and serve immediately.

TOM KAI GAI

➤ **SERVES 4** • PREPARATION: 10 MINUTES • COOKING: 10 MINUTES ⬅

2-inch piece fresh galangal
2 lemongrass stalks, sliced
3½ cups coconut milk

3 small red chiles, halved
4 kaffir lime leaves, torn
10 oz chicken breast, thinly sliced

2 tablespoons fish sauce
2 tablespoons lime juice
2 tablespoons fresh cilantro leaves
(optional)

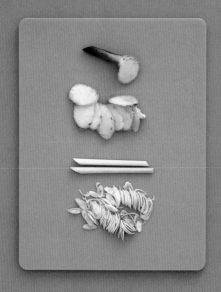

1 2
3 4

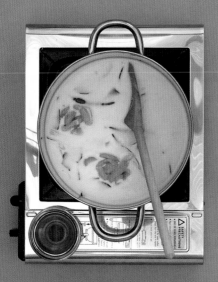

1	Cut the galangal and lemongrass into thin slices.	2	Put the coconut milk in a pan, add the galangal, lemongrass, chiles, and lime leaves and simmer for 5 minutes.
3	Add the chicken meat and fish sauce and cook for 5 minutes, or until the chicken is tender.	4	Remove from the heat and stir in the lime juice and cilantro, if using.

CHICKEN AND CORN SOUP

➤ **SERVES 4–6** • **PREPARATION: 5–8 MINUTES** • **COOKING: 5 MINUTES** ➤

3 corn cobs
2 x 14 oz cans creamed corn
10 oz chicken breast, diced

4 cups chicken bouillon
3 eggs
½ cup evaporated milk

sea salt
½ teaspoon white pepper
2 scallions, finely sliced

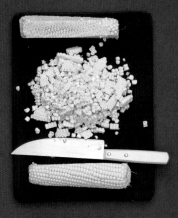

1	Remove the corn from the cobs.	2	Bring the corn, chicken, and bouillon to a boil, then reduce the heat to a simmer.	3	Beat the eggs in a bowl.
4	Gently stir in the eggs, allowing them to form thin threads. Cook for 1 minute.	5	Add the evaporated milk and season with salt and white pepper.	6	Sprinkle with scallions before serving.

MISO SOUP

⟡ **SERVES 4** • PREPARATION: 10 MINUTES + 10 MINUTES SOAKING • COOKING: 10 MINUTES ⟡

3½ oz silken tofu
1 tablespoon wakame (seaweed)
1 teaspoon dashi granules

3 tablespoons red miso (shiro miso)
2 scallions, finely sliced

1
4

2
5

3
6

1	Cut the tofu into small cubes with a sharp knife.	2	Soak the wakame in cold water for 10 minutes, then drain well.	3	Cook the dashi and wakame in 4 cups boiling water for 10 minutes.
4	Blend the miso with a little hot bouillon and return to the pan; do not boil.	5	Divide the tofu among 4 serving bowls.	6	Pour over the hot bouillon and garnish with scallions. Serve immediately.

PHO BO

⤞ SERVES 4–6 • PREPARATION: 20 MINUTES • COOKING: 1 HOUR ⤝

6 cups beef bouillon
1¼ oz fresh gingerroot, sliced
2 onions, halved
2 cinnamon sticks
2 star anise

3 cloves
1 teaspoon black peppercorns
3 tablespoons fish sauce
1¼ lb fresh rice noodles
3½ oz bean sprouts

7 oz beef fillet, very thinly sliced
2 scallions, sliced
2 tablespoons fresh cilantro
lime wedges and finely cracked black
pepper, to serve

1 2
3 4

1	Bring the bouillon, gingerroot, onions, spices, peppercorns, and fish sauce to a boil, then lower the heat and cook, covered, for 30 minutes.	2	Strain and discard the seasonings, then return the bouillon to the pan and bring back to a boil.
3	Put the noodles, bean sprouts, and sliced beef into serving bowls.	4	Ladle over the bouillon, top with scallions and cilantro, and serve with lime wedges and cracked black pepper.

GOI CUON

⇟ MAKES 8 • PREPARATION: 30 MINUTES • COOKING: NIL ⇞

3 oz dried rice vermicelli
8 rice paper rounds, 8½ inches in diameter
½ cup finely shredded lettuce

16 fresh mint leaves
16 cooked shrimp, peeled and deveined

DIPPING SAUCE:
2 tablespoons fish sauce
1 tablespoon lime juice
2 tablespoons sweet chili sauce

1 2 3
4 5 6

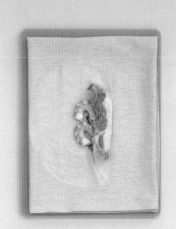

1	Put the vermicelli in a bowl and cover with boiling water. Leave for 5 minutes.	2	Rinse and drain well.	3	Soak 1 rice paper round in cold water until soft.	
4	Put on paper towels, then lay 1 heaping tablespoon each of vermicelli, lettuce, and mint on top. Roll once.	5	Top with 2 shrimp.	6	Fold in the sides and roll up carefully to enclose the filling.	➤

7	Transfer to a plate and cover with damp paper towels while you prepare the remaining rolls.	**VEGETARIAN ALTERNATIVE** ❋ Use sliced firm tofu instead of the shrimp.

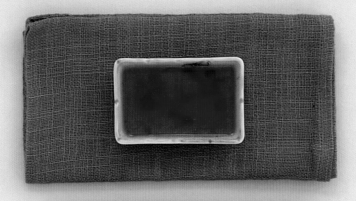

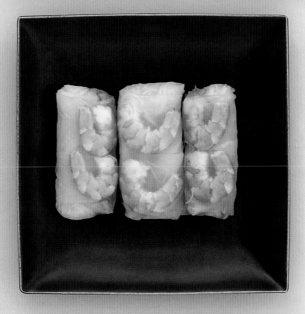

8

For the dipping sauce, put all the ingredients in a bowl and mix to combine. Serve with the rolls.

SERVING SUGGESTION
❋

These rolls are also delicious served with a hoisin sauce topped with chopped peanuts.

NEMS

➤ **MAKES 8 • PREPARATION: 30 MINUTES • COOKING: 20 MINUTES** ➤

3 oz dried mung bean vermicelli
6 dried shiitake mushrooms
1 carrot, finely shredded
5 oz ground pork
1 tablespoon chopped fresh cilantro

8 rice paper rounds, 8½ inches in diameter
peanut oil, for deep-frying
shredded Chinese cabbage, to serve
DIPPING SAUCE:
1 tablespoon fish sauce

3 tablespoons lime juice
1 garlic clove, chopped
1 small red chili, deseeded and finely chopped
1 teaspoon superfine sugar

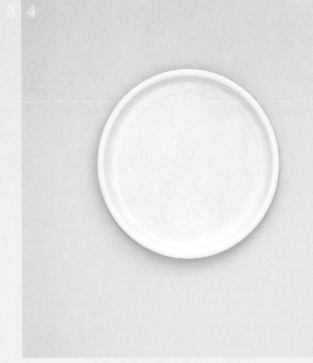

1	Put the noodles in a bowl, cover with boiling water, and leave for 5 minutes. Rinse and drain, then cut into shorter lengths using scissors.	2	Soak the mushrooms in boiling water for 10 minutes, or until soft. Drain, then remove and discard the stalks. Finely chop the caps.
3	Put the noodles, mushrooms, carrot, pork, and cilantro in a bowl and mix well to combine.	4	Soak 1 rice paper round in a dish of cold water until soft. ➤

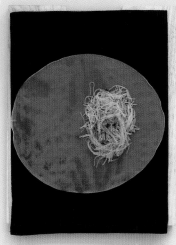

5	Place on a clean kitchen towel. Put 2 heaping tablespoons of the noodle mixture on top.	6	Fold in the sides and roll up to enclose the filling. Repeat with the remaining rice papers and filling.
7	Heat the oil and deep-fry the rolls in batches until crisp and golden. Drain on paper towels.	8	To make the dipping sauce, put all the ingredients in a bowl and mix to combine.

9 Arrange the rolls on a bed of shredded cabbage and serve with the dipping sauce.

VARIATION
❋

Substitute ground chicken for the pork.

SERVING SUGGESTION
❋

These rolls are delicious sliced into 3 pieces and served on top of noodles. (See Bo Bun, recipe 28, and replace the beef with the sliced nems.)

DIM SUM

❧ **MAKES 14 • PREPARATION: 40 MINUTES • COOKING: 15 MINUTES** ❧

8 oz ground pork
2 oz canned water chestnuts, chopped
1 tablespoon light soy sauce

1 tablespoon Shaoxing rice wine
½ teaspoon sesame oil
1 scallion, sliced
1 tablespoon shredded fresh gingerroot

14 wonton wrappers (square)
choice of dipping sauce, to serve

1 2
3 4

1	Put the pork, chestnuts, soy sauce, rice wine, sesame oil, scallion, and gingerroot into a bowl and mix to combine.	2	Put a tablespoon of the filling into the center of a wonton wrapper. Gather up the edges to enclose the sides of the filling, leaving the top open. Repeat with the remaining wrappers.
3	Put the wontons in a steamer. Cover and cook over simmering water for 15 minutes.	4	Serve with your choice of dipping sauce.

EDAMAME

❧ **SERVES 4** • PREPARATION: 5 MINUTES • COOKING: 10 MINUTES ❧

1 lb frozen soy beans in the pod
2 tablespoons soy sauce
2 tablespoons rice vinegar
1 teaspoon shredded fresh gingerroot

1 2
3 4

1	Cook the soy beans in a large pan of boiling water for 5 minutes, or until bright green and soft.	2	Rinse under cold running water and drain well.
3	For the dipping sauce, mix the soy sauce, rice vinegar, and gingerroot together.	4	Serve the soybeans in their pods accompanied by bowls of the sauce.

GYOZA

⇝ MAKES 30 • PREPARATION: 30 MINUTES • COOKING: 15 MINUTES ⇜

12 oz ground pork
¾ cup shredded Chinese cabbage
2 scallions, sliced
2 teaspoons shredded fresh gingerroot
1 egg, lightly beaten

1 tablespoon soy sauce
2 teaspoons mirin
2 teaspoons sake
30 gyoza wrappers, or as needed
2 tablespoons vegetable oil

DIPPING SAUCE:
2 tablespoons soy sauce
2 tablespoons rice vinegar

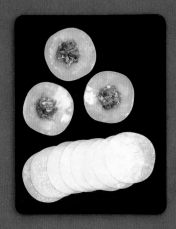

| 1 | Mix together the pork, cabbage, scallions, gingerroot, egg, soy sauce, mirin, and sake. | 2 | Lay gyoza wrappers on a board and put 2 teaspoons of the filling into the center of each. | 3 | Brush the edges of the wrappers lightly with water. | |
| 4 | Bring the edges together and pinch to seal. Repeat with all the wrappers. | 5 | Heat the oil in a skillet and add enough gyoza to cover the base. Cook until crisp. | 6 | Add ½ cup water, cover, and cook for 5 minutes. | ➤ |

7	For the dipping sauce, mix the soy sauce and rice vinegar together.

TIP
※

Gyoza can be made ahead of time and frozen, uncooked, in an airtight container until ready to use.

VARIATION
※

For something different, try steaming or deep-frying the gyoza.

8   Serve the gyoza warm with the dipping sauce.

SERVING SUGGESTION
❊

Gyoza are delicious added to noodle soups. Cook as per the recipe and then float them on the top of Japanese udon soups.

VARIATION
❊

Try adding some finely chopped raw vegetables to the mixture, such as shiitake mushrooms, shredded carrot, shredded daikon (white radish), or some shredded spinach.

CALIFORNIA ROLLS

➤ **SERVES 4** • PREPARATION: 20 MINUTES • COOKING: 20 MINUTES ◆

4–6 sheets roasted nori (seaweed)
2½ cups cooked seasoned sushi rice (see recipe 03)

2 tablespoons Japanese mayonnaise
8 crabsticks
1 avocado, cut into thin strips

TO SERVE:
soy sauce
wasabi

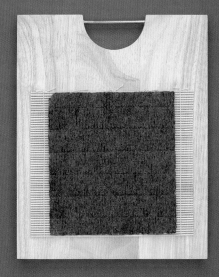

1 2
3 4

1	Put 1 sheet of nori onto a bamboo mat.	2	Spread the rice over two-thirds of the mat.	
3	Squeeze a line of mayonnaise over the center of the rice.	4	Top with the crabsticks and avocado.	➤

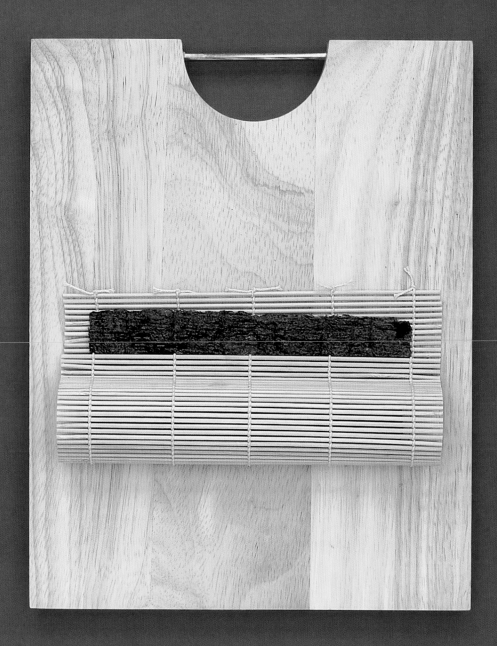

5	Roll up to enclose the filling, drawing the mat tight as you roll.

VARIATION
❖

Try substituting some sliced raw (sushi-grade) salmon or tuna for the crabsticks.

VARIATIONS
❖

Other ideas for sushi rolls include cooked teryaki chicken, deep-fried vegetables, seaweed salad, pickled daikon (white radish), and finely shredded carrot, cucumber, and tofu.

6	Using a sharp knife, cut the roll in half, then into thirds. Serve with soy sauce and wasabi.

TIP
※

To keep any leftover nori sheets fresh, store them in an airtight container.

TIP
※

Sushi rolls can be made ahead of time, but do not slice them until you are ready to serve.

FISH CAKES

❧ MAKES 24 • PREPARATION: 15 MINUTES • COOKING: 20 MINUTES ❧

1 lb boneless white fish fillets, chopped
2 tablespoons red curry paste
1 egg
3½ oz snake beans, thinly sliced

4 kaffir lime leaves, finely shredded
peanut oil, for deep-frying
DIPPING SAUCE:
1 small red chili, chopped

½ cucumber, finely chopped
1 tablespoon chopped fresh cilantro
1 tablespoon white granulated sugar
½ cup white rice vinegar

1

2

3

4

5

6

1	Put the fish, curry paste, and egg into a food-mixer and process until smooth.	2	Transfer the mixture to a bowl, add the snake beans and lime leaves, and mix to combine.	3	Shape tablespoons of the mixture into flat patties.
4	Heat the oil in a wok and deep-fry the fish cakes in batches until golden. Drain.	5	For the dipping sauce, combine all the ingredients in a bowl.	6	Serve the fish cakes with the dipping sauce.

SHRIMP TOAST

→ MAKES 18 • PREPARATION: 15 MINUTES • COOKING: 20 MINUTES ←

10 slices white bread
1 lb 10 oz green king shrimp, peeled and deveined (gives 12 oz shrimp meat)
2 teaspoons shredded fresh gingerroot

2 teaspoons cornstarch
1 egg white
2 teaspoons Shaoxing rice wine (optional)
2 tablespoons chopped fresh cilantro

1 scallion, sliced
4 tablespoons sesame seeds
peanut oil, for deep-frying
sweet chili sauce or soy sauce, to serve

1
4

2
5

3
6

1	Remove the crusts from the bread slices and cut them in half to make rectangles.	2	Put the shrimp, gingerroot, cornstarch, egg white, and rice wine into a food-mixer.	
3	Process until the mixture forms a smooth paste.			
4	Transfer to a bowl and stir in the cilantro and scallion.	5	Spread the shrimp mixture over the bread and sprinkle with sesame seeds.	
6	Heat the oil and fry the toasts in batches until crisp. Serve with the sauce.			

SASHIMI

❧ **SERVES 4** • PREPARATION: 15 MINUTES • COOKING: 5 MINUTES ❦

7 oz sushi-grade tuna
7 oz sushi-grade salmon fillet
7 oz very fresh scallops

1 daikon (white radish), scrubbed
1 carrot
½ teaspoon wasabi

TOSA DIPPING SAUCE:
3 tablespoons mirin
⅓ cup soy sauce

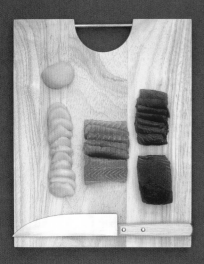

1 2
3 4

1	Cut the tuna, salmon, and scallops into ½-inch thick slices.	2	For the dipping sauce, bring the mirin and soy sauce to a boil over a high heat for 5 minutes. Let cool.
3	Using a mandolin or sharp knife, finely shred the daikon (white radish) and carrot.	4	Mound the vegetables onto the serving plate beside the fish and serve with the dipping sauce and wasabi.

CHICKEN SATAY

❧ **SERVES 4** • PREPARATION: 20 MINUTES + 15 MINUTES SOAKING • COOKING: 25 MINUTES ❧

1 lb chicken breast fillet

SATAY SAUCE:
¼ cup peanuts
1 cup coconut milk
2 tablespoons red curry paste

1–2 tablespoons shredded palm sugar
1 tablespoon tamarind concentrate (paste)

1
4

2
5

3
6

1	Soak several bamboo skewers for 15 minutes. Cut the chicken into cubes.	2	Thread the chicken onto the presoaked skewers.	3	For the sauce, dry-fry the peanuts, then crush them in a food-mixer.
4	Heat the milk, add the nuts and remaining ingredients, and cook for 15 minutes.	5	Griddle or chargrill the chicken until tender, turning during cooking.	6	Serve the chicken with the satay sauce.

MEAT

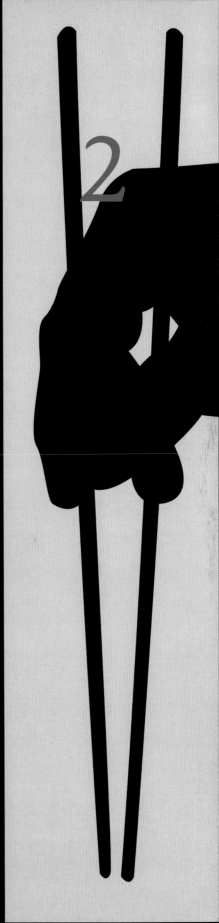

STIR-FRIES

GRILLS & ROASTS

CLASSICS

CURRIES

LARB MOO

❧ **SERVES 4** • **PREPARATION: 10 MINUTES** • **COOKING: 15 MINUTES** ❧

1 lb ground pork
¼ teaspoon chili powder
2 tablespoons chopped red shallots
or red onions
1 tablespoon finely chopped lemongrass

3 tablespoons fish sauce
3 tablespoons lime juice
2 tablespoons chopped fresh mint
2 tablespoons chopped fresh cilantro

TO SERVE
1 Boston lettuce, separated into leaves
lime wedges

1 2
3 4

1	Put the pork, chili powder, shallots, and lemongrass in a bowl and mix to combine.	2	Heat the wok over a high heat, add the pork mixture, and stir-fry until the pork is cooked but not browned.
3	Turn off the heat and stir in the fish sauce, lime juice, mint, and cilantro.	4	Serve warm with lettuce leaves and lime wedges.

SUNG CHOI BAU

⇾ **SERVES 4** • PREPARATION: 20 MINUTES + 10 MINUTES STANDING • COOKING: 20 MINUTES ⇽

1 iceberg lettuce
4 dry shiitake mushrooms
1 tablespoon peanut oil
½ teaspoon sesame oil

1 lb fatty ground pork
2 garlic cloves, chopped
2¼ oz can water chestnuts, rinsed, drained, and chopped

4 tablespoons oyster sauce
2 tablespoons Shaoxing rice wine
1 teaspoon superfine sugar
2 scallions, sliced

1 2
3 4

1	Remove the core from the lettuce.	2	Gently separate the leaves from the lettuce and trim to form small cups.	
3	Put the mushrooms in a bowl, cover with boiling water, and leave for 10 minutes, or until soft. Discard the stems. Finely chop the caps.	4	Heat the oils in a wok, add the pork, and stir-fry for 3 minutes, or until browned.	➢

5	Add the garlic and water chestnuts and stir-fry for 3 minutes. Add the oyster sauce, rice wine, sugar, and scallions and bring to a boil. Cook over a high heat for 5 minutes, or until the sauce reduces slightly.

VARIATION
❋

Use ground beef or chicken instead of the pork.

TIP
❋

Try topping the sung choi bau with crispy fried egg noodles for some extra crunch.

6

Serve the meat in bowls with the lettuce leaves—invite each person to fill their own leaves with the meat filling.

You can serve the sung choi bau either hot or cold. They are also good served as an appetizer at parties in baby cos leaves.

BEEF IN BLACK BEAN SAUCE

❧ **SERVES 4** • PREPARATION: 20 MINUTES + 30 MINUTES MARINATING • COOKING: 10 MINUTES ❧

1 lb beef fillet, cut into thin strips
1 tablespoon light soy sauce
1 tablespoon Shaoxing rice wine
2 tablespoons peanut oil
½ teaspoon sesame oil

1 onion, sliced
2 garlic cloves, sliced
1 red bell pepper, sliced
1 green bell pepper, sliced

4 tablespoons salted black beans, rinsed
and chopped
1 teaspoon superfine sugar
4 tablespoons oyster sauce
freshly cooked rice, to serve

1	Mix the beef, soy sauce, and rice wine together in a non-metallic bowl.	2	Heat the oils in a wok, add the onion and garlic, and stir-fry for 3 minutes.	3	Add the beef and stir-fry for 5 minutes, or until the meat is tender.
4	Add the sliced red and green bell peppers.	5	Add the black beans, sugar, and oyster sauce to the wok and stir-fry for 2 minutes.	6	Serve the beef with freshly cooked rice.

YAKI SOBA

⇾ SERVES 4 • PREPARATION: 15 MINUTES • COOKING: 15 MINUTES ⇽

1 tablespoon vegetable oil
10 oz pork fillet, thinly sliced
13 oz fresh hokkien noodles
7 oz peeled cooked shrimp

7 oz Chinese cabbage, finely shredded
3 scallions, sliced
1 red bell pepper, thinly sliced
3 tablespoons light soy sauce

1 tablespoon superfine sugar
1 egg, lightly beaten
pickled ginger, to serve

1 2 3
4 5 6

1	Heat 2 teaspoons of the oil in a pan, add the pork, and cook until browned.	2	Cook the noodles in hot water for 3 minutes, then drain well.	3	Mix the pork, noodles, shrimp, vegetables, soy, sugar, and egg together.
4	Heat the remaining oil in a wok until it starts to smoke, then add the noodle mixture.	5	Stir-fry until everything is heated through and the egg is cooked.	6	Serve the noodles topped with pickled ginger.

SHAKING BEEF

✤ **SERVES 4** • PREPARATION: 15 MINUTES + 30 MINUTES MARINATING • COOKING: 10 MINUTES ✤

5 Asian shallots
4 tablespoons white vinegar
1 tablespoon superfine sugar
1 tablespoon fish sauce

4 garlic cloves, chopped
2 tablespoons vegetable oil
1 lb rump steak, cut into small cubes

1¾ oz butter
1 Boston lettuce, separated into leaves

1 2
3 4

1	Peel and thinly slice the shallots, put into the vinegar with 2 tablespoons of water and leave for 30 minutes.	2	Put the sugar, fish sauce, garlic, 1 tablespoon of oil, and the steak, into a bowl.
3	Heat the remaining oil and the butter in a wok over a high heat, add the beef and cook until browned but still pink in the center.	4	Drain the shallots and divide among the lettuce leaves on a serving plate. Top with the cooked beef and serve.

CHAR SUI PORK

SERVES 4–6 • PREPARATION: 15 MINUTES + 2–8 HOURS MARINATING • COOKING: 30 MINUTES

2 garlic cloves, chopped
1 tablespoon shredded fresh gingerroot
1 tablespoon malt vinegar
¼ cup Shaoxing rice wine
¼ cup hoisin sauce

¼ cup Chinese barbecue sauce
1 tablespoon light soy sauce
1 lb pork shoulder, cut into large pieces
1½ tablespoons honey

TO SERVE:
freshly cooked rice
steamed Asian greens, such as bok choi

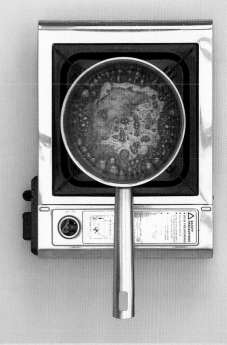

1 2
3 4

1	Whisk the garlic, ginger, vinegar, rice wine, hoisin, barbecue sauce, and soy sauce together in a bowl. Pour over the pork, then cover and chill for 2 hours, or overnight.	2	Preheat the oven to 475°F. Arrange the pork pieces on a wire rack over a roasting pan half-filled with water.
3	Bake for 30 minutes, basting several times with the marinade, until the pork is tender.	4	Put the honey in a pan and bring to a boil. ➤

5	Brush the honey over the pork and set aside to cool.

TIP

❋

The longer you leave the pork in its marinade the more intense the flavor will be.

SERVING SUGGESTION

❋

The cooked sliced pork is delicious added to stir-fries with noodles and vegetables.

6	Slice the pork and serve with freshly cooked rice and Asian greens.

TIP
❋

Use the cooked pork in rice paper rolls or sushi.

SERVING SUGGESTION
❋

Serve the sliced pork on top of wonton noodle soups.

SESAME BEEF SALAD

✤ **SERVES 4** • PREPARATION: 10 MINUTES + 10 MINUTES RESTING • COOKING: 5 MINUTES ✤

1 lb rump steak
1 tablespoon vegetable oil
5 oz mizuna leaves
3 scallions
2 tablespoons sesame seeds, toasted

DRESSING:
3 tablespoons light soy sauce
3 tablespoons lemon juice
1 teaspoon superfine sugar
1 garlic clove, chopped very finely

½ teaspoon sesame oil
1 teaspoon shredded fresh gingerroot

1	Mix together all the ingredients for the dressing.	2	Rub both sides of the steak with the oil, then chargrill for 3 minutes on each side, or until cooked rare.	3	Loosely cover the steak with aluminum foil and rest for 10 minutes.
4	Cut the steak into thin slices with a sharp knife.	5	Arrange the mizuna leaves, onions, and steak on a plate.	6	Pour over the dressing and sprinkle with sesame seeds.

BUN CHA

⊱ SERVES 4 • PREPARATION: 20 MINUTES + 4 HOURS MARINATING • COOKING: 20 MINUTES ⊰

1 tablespoon shredded palm sugar
2 tablespoons fish sauce
2 garlic cloves, chopped
2 Asian shallots, chopped
1 lb ground pork
7 oz dry rice noodles

DIPPING SAUCE:
4 tablespoons fish sauce
6 tablespoons lime juice
2 teaspoons superfine sugar
2 red chiles, seeded and finely chopped

TO SERVE:
3½ oz bean sprouts
fresh cilantro and mint sprigs
lettuce leaves

1	Put the sugar and fish sauce into a small pan and stir over a low heat until the sugar melts. Cool.	2	Put the cooled sauce, garlic, shallots, and pork into a bowl and mix to combine. Marinate for 4 hours.	3	Shape the mixture into patties—use 2 tablespoons to get the shape.
4	Chargrill the patties until slightly charred and tender.	5	Mix the sauce ingredients. Cook the noodles in boiling water until soft. Drain.	6	Serve the patties on the noodles with the sauce, sprouts, herbs, and lettuce.

BABI KETJAP

❧ **SERVES 4** • **PREPARATION: 10 MINUTES + 30 MINUTES MARINATING** • **COOKING: 15 MINUTES** ❧

1 lb pork fillet
2 tablespoons all-purpose flour
1 tablespoon soy sauce
½ teaspoon powdered ginger

3 tablespoons vegetable oil
1 onion, finely chopped
3 garlic cloves, chopped
2-inch piece fresh gingerroot, shredded

½ cup kecap manis
1 teaspoon chili powder
1 tablespoon lemon juice
freshly cooked rice, to serve

1 2
3 4

1	Cut the pork into small cubes. Put the flour, soy sauce, and ginger into a bowl and mix well. Mix in the pork and chill for 30 minutes.	2	Heat the oil in a wok, add the meat in batches, and cook until browned.
3	Add the onion, garlic, and fresh gingerroot and cook until soft.	4	Add the kecap manis, chili, and 3 tablespoons of water and cook for 5 minutes until thick. Stir in the lemon juice and serve with rice.

BO BUN

➤ **SERVES 4 • PREPARATION: 15 MINUTES + 30 MINUTES MARINATING • COOKING: 10 MINUTES** ←

4 tablespoons fish sauce
3 tablespoons shredded palm sugar
7 oz dry vermicelli
2 tablespoons soy sauce
2 tablespoons oyster sauce

2 teaspoons curry powder
1 garlic clove, crushed
2 sticks lemongrass, thinly sliced
1 lb beef fillet, cut into thin strips
2 tablespoons vegetable oil

1 carrot + ½ cucumber, julienned
3½ oz bean sprouts
½ cup fresh mint leaves
½ cup fresh cilantro
3½ oz roasted peanuts, crushed

1	Put the fish sauce, 2 tablespoons of water, and the palm sugar into a small pan and cook over a low heat until the sugar dissolves. Cool.	2	Cook the noodles in boiling water for 3–5 minutes, or until soft. Drain well, then set aside in cold water.
3	Put the soy sauce, oyster sauce, curry powder, garlic, and lemongrass in a bowl, add the beef, and mix. Cover and marinate for 30 minutes.	4	Heat the oil in a wok over a high heat and cook the meat in batches until it is browned. ➤

5 Divide the well-drained noodles among 4 serving plates. Top with the carrot, cucumber, bean sprouts, mint, and cilantro.	**VARIATION** ❈ Try cooking the meat on the grill or chargrill on a ridged griddle to add a more traditional flavor.
TIP ❈ For extra flavor, allow the meat to marinate overnight in the fridge.	

6	Divide the meat among the plates. Sprinkle with crushed peanuts and drizzle with the cooled fish sauce and sugar mixture.

TIP
❈

This dish is delicious served either hot or cold.

VARIATION
❈

You can use lamb instead of the beef, if you prefer.

PORK TONKATSU

❧ **SERVES 4** • PREPARATION: 20 MINUTES • COOKING: 10 MINUTES ❧

4 pork loin steaks
1 cup all-purpose flour
2 eggs, lightly beaten
1 cup panko (Japanese bread crumbs)

peanut oil, for shallow-frying
2 cups shredded cabbage
1 lemon, cut into wedges

TONKATSU SAUCE
1¼ fl oz tomato ketchup
¼ cup Worcestershire sauce

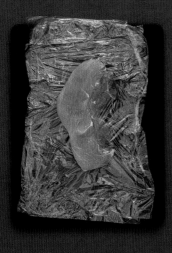

1

2

3

4

5

6

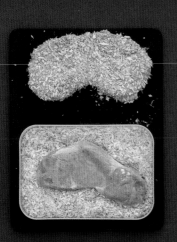

1	Put one of the pork loin steaks between 2 sheets of plastic wrap.	2	Pound using a meat mallet until ¼ inch thick. Repeat with the other steaks.	3	Dust both sides of each steak lightly with flour, shaking off any excess.
4	Dip the steaks into the beaten egg and press to coat in the bread crumbs.	5	Heat the oil in a skillet, add the pork, and cook for 3 minutes on each side, or until crisp. Drain.	6	Mix the ketchup and Worcestershire sauce. Serve with sliced pork, cabbage, and lemon wedges.

MASAMAN BEEF

⇴ SERVES 4 • PREPARATION: 20 MINUTES • COOKING: 25 MINUTES ⇴

2 potatoes
1 tablespoon vegetable oil
3 tablespoons Masaman curry paste
1 lb rump steak, cubed

1 onion, chopped
2 cups coconut milk
2 tablespoons shredded palm sugar
2 tablespoons fish sauce

3 tablespoons tamarind concentrate (paste)
3 tablespoons roasted peanuts, chopped
steamed jasmine rice, to serve

1 2 3
4 5 6

1	Cut the potatoes into large pieces then steam or parboil.	2	Heat the oil in a wok, add the curry paste, and cook gently for 3 minutes, or until fragrant.	3	Increase the heat to medium. Add the potatoes, steak, and onion, and cook until the steak browns.
4	Stir in the milk, sugar, and fish sauce. Boil, then simmer for 10 minutes.	5	Add the tamarind and cook for a further 5 minutes.	6	Top with the chopped roasted peanuts and serve with steamed jasmine rice.

BEEF RENDANG

⇢ **SERVES 6** • PREPARATION: 20 MINUTES + 30 MINUTES MARINATING • COOKING: 1¾ HOURS ⇠

2 oz large dry red chiles
1 teaspoon coriander seeds
1 tablespoon chopped fresh gingerroot
2 teaspoons powdered cumin
½ teaspoon powdered cloves

¼ teaspoon turmeric
3 garlic cloves
10 red Asian shallots, roughly chopped
2 lb beef topside, cubed
⅓ cup flaked coconut

2 cups coconut milk
2 stalks lemongrass
1 tablespoon chopped galangal
2 teaspoons shredded palm sugar
freshly cooked rice, to serve

1

4

2

5

3

6

1	Soak the chiles in boiling water for 15 minutes, or until soft. Drain well and roughly chop.	2	Put the chiles, coriander seeds, ginger, cumin, cloves, turmeric, garlic, and shallots into a food-mixer.	3	Process to a smooth paste (you may need to add a little water to bring the paste together).
4	Put the meat into a bowl, add the spice paste, and mix. Chill for 30 minutes.	5	Put the meat, coconut, coconut milk, lemongrass, galangal, and sugar in a wok.	6	Bring to a boil, then lower the heat and simmer for 1½ hours. ➤

7	Continue to cook, stirring continuously, until the curry is dry.	**TIP**
		The flavor of this dish improves on standing so it is best made the day before.
		VARIATION
		This is a great recipe to cook in a pressure cooker; allow 20 minutes to cook.

8	Serve with freshly cooked rice.	**VARIATION** ❈
		This is a mild rendang so if you would like it spicier add some extra dry red chiles to the paste.
	TIP ❈	**SERVING SUGGESTION** ❈
	Rendang is a dry dish so be sure to cook the meat until there is hardly any liquid left.	Rendang makes a tasty filling for pies; serve mini pies at a buffet.

JAPANESE BEEF CURRY

⋟ **SERVES 4** • PREPARATION: 15 MINUTES • COOKING: 20 MINUTES ⋞

1 tablespoon vegetable oil
1 lb rump steak, cubed
1 onion, chopped
2 potatoes, cut into bite-sized pieces

1 carrot, cut into thick slices
1 packet Japanese pork curry mix, crumbled
freshly cooked rice, to serve

1	Heat the oil in a pan, add the steak, and cook until browned. Add the onion and cook over a medium heat for 5 minutes until golden.	2	Add the potatoes, carrot, and 2 cups water, cover, and simmer for 10 minutes, or until the vegetables are soft.
3	Add the crumbled curry mix and cook, stirring, for 5 minutes, or until the sauce is smooth and thickened.	4	Serve with freshly cooked rice.

POULTRY

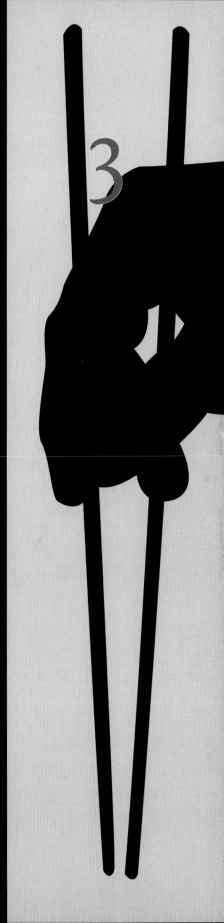

NOODLE DISHES

COCONUT MILK DISHES

STIR-FRIES

CLASSICS

SPICY FRIED CHICKEN

❧ **SERVES 4** • PREPARATION: 15 MINUTES • COOKING: 15 MINUTES ❧

1¼ lb cooked udon noodles
1 tablespoon vegetable oil
10 oz chicken thigh fillets, sliced
3 scallions, sliced

1 red bell pepper, sliced
7 oz shiitake mushrooms, sliced
1 bunch bok choi, roughly chopped
3½ oz bean sprouts

2 tablespoons sake
3 tablespoons light soy sauce
3 tablespoons sweet chili sauce
½ teaspoon chili flakes

1

4

2

5

3

6

1	Gently separate the noodles.	2	Heat the oil in a wok, add the chicken, and cook until it has browned.	3	Add the onions, bell pepper, and mushrooms and cook for 3 minutes.
4	Add the noodles, bok choi, and bean sprouts and toss to combine.	5	Mix the sake, sauces, and chili flakes together. Add to the wok and toss to coat until heated through.	6	Serve immediately.

CHILI CHICKEN RAMEN

➤ SERVES 4 • PREPARATION: 5 MINUTES • COOKING: 10 MINUTES ➤

2 chicken breast fillets
1 teaspoon vegetable oil
1 tablespoon chili sauce
7oz dry ramen or 2-minute noodles

1 bunch bok choi, roughly chopped
4 cups hot chicken bouillon
3 scallions, sliced

1	Brush the chicken with oil. Chargrill, basting with the chili sauce, until tender.	2	Remove the chicken and rest it for 5 minutes before cutting into thick slices.	3	Cook the noodles in hot water for 2–3 minutes, or until tender.
4	Drain the noodles and divide among 4 bowls.	5	Add the bok choi to the noodles and pour over the hot bouillon.	6	Arrange the chicken and scallions on top and serve.

CHICKEN PAD THAI

SERVES 4 • PREPARATION: 30 MINUTES + 15 MINUTES STANDING • COOKING: 15 MINUTES

10 oz dry rice stick noodles
2 tablespoons vegetable oil
10 oz chicken breast fillets, sliced
3½ oz firm tofu, sliced
3 garlic cloves, chopped

2 tablespoons dry shrimp (optional)
½ cup fish sauce
2 tablespoons superfine sugar
⅓ cup tamarind juice
3 eggs, lightly beaten

3 tablespoons chopped roasted peanuts
2 tablespoons garlic chives, cut into
1¼-inch pieces
2 cups bean sprouts
1 lime, cut into wedges

1 2
3 4

1	Put the noodles into a bowl and cover with cold water. Leave for 15 minutes, or until just soft. Drain well.	2	Heat the oil in a wok, add the chicken and tofu, and stir-fry over a high heat for 5 minutes, or until the chicken is browned.
3	Add the garlic and shrimp, if using, and cook for 2 minutes.	4	Add the noodles. Mix the fish sauce, sugar, and tamarind with ½ cup water, add to the wok, and cook for 5 minutes. ➤

5	Push the noodles up one side of the wok, add the eggs, and cook, stirring, until the eggs are scrambled. Add the peanuts and chives and combine with the noodles and eggs.

TIP
❈

Make sure you soak the noodles in cold water. If you use hot water they will become too soft.

VEGETARIAN ALTERNATIVE
❈

To make vegetarian pad Thai increase the tofu and omit the chicken and shrimp. Replace the fish sauce with light soy sauce.

6	Stir-fry for 2 minutes. Add the bean sprouts and toss to combine. Serve with lime wedges.	**SERVING SUGGESTION** ⁕ Use 9 oz chopped peeled fresh shrimp if you want to make this dish for a dinner party.
	TIP ⁕ To reheat any leftover pad Thai add a few tablespoons of water to the wok along with the noodles. This will stop them sticking to the wok.	**TIP** ⁕ Be sure to stir-fry the noodles in step 4 until soft.

DUCK & PINEAPPLE CURRY

❧ SERVES 4 • PREPARATION: 15 MINUTES • COOKING: 20 MINUTES ❧

7 fl oz coconut milk, including the thick cream at the top of the can (do not shake the can before opening)
2–3 tablespoons red curry paste

1 roast duck, cut into pieces
8 oz pineapple, cut into bite-sized pieces
1 red bell pepper, chopped
1 tablespoon fish sauce

1 tablespoon shredded palm sugar
2 tablespoons fresh Thai basil leaves

1 2
3 4

1	Scoop the thick coconut cream from the top of the can into a wok and cook until the oil begins to separate from the cream.	2	Add the curry paste and cook for 5 minutes, or until fragrant.
3	Add the coconut milk, duck, pineapple, bell pepper, fish sauce, and sugar and cook for 15 minutes.	4	Scatter with basil leaves before serving.

GREEN CURRY PASTE

MAKES ¼ CUP • PREPARATION: 5–15 MINUTES • COOKING: 3 MINUTES

½ teaspoon cumin seeds
½ teaspoon coriander seeds
1 star anise
½ teaspoon white peppercorns
1 teaspoon salt

3 garlic cloves
4 lemongrass stalks, peeled
1–2 knobs of fresh galangal
2–3 fresh cilantro roots, cleaned
8 Asian shallots, chopped

1 small green chili + 6 large green chiles
½ cup fresh cilantro leaves
vegetable oil, to cover

1 2
3 4

1	Put the cumin seeds, coriander seeds, star anise, and peppercorns in a skillet and cook for 3 minutes, or until fragrant.	2	Transfer to a food-mixer add the salt, garlic, lemongrass, galangal, cilantro roots, shallots, chiles, and coriander leaves.
3	Process the mixture to form a smooth paste, scraping down the sides a couple of times.	4	Transfer the paste to a bowl, cover with a little vegetable oil, and cover with plastic wrap until ready to use.

CHICKEN GREEN CURRY

➤ SERVES 4 • PREPARATION: 15 MINUTES • COOKING: 20 MINUTES ◄

4 kaffir lime leaves
1 tablespoon palm sugar (optional)
1 tablespoon vegetable oil
2–3 tablespoons green curry paste

2 cups coconut milk
1 lb chicken thigh fillets
6 small round pea eggplants, quartered
1 tablespoon fish sauce

2 tablespoons fresh Thai basil leaves
freshly cooked rice, to serve

1 2
3 4

1	Finely shred the lime leaves and the palm sugar, if using.	2	Heat the oil in a skillet, add the curry paste, and cook until the oil separates from the curry paste.	
3	Add the coconut milk and cook for 5 minutes.	4	Add the chicken, eggplants, and lime leaves and simmer for 10 minutes, or until the chicken is tender.	➤

5	Season with fish sauce and the palm sugar.	**TIP** ❀ Curry freezes well. Put it in an airtight container and label with the date. It will keep for 6 weeks.
	VARIATION ❀ Any fresh vegetables can be used in this curry, such as snake beans, baby corn, cauliflower, or broccoli.	

6	Top the curry with the basil leaves and serve with freshly cooked rice.

TIP
❋

The flavor of curry improves on standing so if you can, make it the day before or in the morning.

TIP
❋

Green curry paste is hotter than red and commercial curry pastes can be quite fiery. I recommend tasting a little bit to gauge its heat—you can always add more at the end if you want it hotter.

VIETNAMESE CHICKEN CURRY

➤ **SERVES 4** • PREPARATION: 15 MINUTES + 3 HOURS MARINATING • COOKING: 50 MINUTES ⬅

1 knob of galangal
3 lemongrass stalks
3 garlic cloves
1 onion

2 tablespoons curry powder
3 lb chicken pieces
2 tablespoons vegetable oil
2 cups coconut milk

1 tablespoon superfine sugar
1 lb potatoes, cut into large pieces
freshly cooked rice, to serve

1 2
3 4

1	Roughly chop the galangal, lemongrass, garlic, and onion.	2	Put the galangal, lemongrass, garlic, onion, and curry powder into a food-mixer and process to form a smooth paste.	
3	Spread the paste over the chicken, cover, and leave to marinate in the fridge for 3 hours.	4	Heat the oil in a large skillet, add the chicken, in batches if necessary, and cook until browned.	➤

5	Add the coconut milk, sugar, 1 cup water, and potatoes. Cover and simmer for 40 minutes, or until the chicken is tender.

VARIATION
❋

You can use all drumsticks for this recipe if you have trouble finding chicken pieces.

TIP
❋

You can buy a whole 3 lb chicken and cut it into pieces, if you prefer.

6	Serve with freshly cooked rice.	**SERVING SUGGESTION** ❋
		If you are not going to serve this dish immediately, do not add the potatoes. Add them when you reheat the curry to stop them overcooking and breaking up.
TIP ❋		
Use a Vietnamese-style curry powder instead of an Indian one, if you can find one.		

STIR-FRIED CHICKEN

⇝ **SERVES 4** • PREPARATION: 15 MINUTES • COOKING: 10 MINUTES ⇜

1 tablespoon vegetable oil
1 lb chicken breast fillets, thinly sliced
2 garlic cloves, chopped
1 large red chili, deseeded and thinly sliced

1 red bell pepper, thinly sliced
3 scallions, sliced
1 tablespoon palm sugar
2 tablespoons chili jam

1 tablespoon fish sauce
½ cup fresh Thai basil leaves
freshly cooked rice, to serve

1 2
3 4

1	Heat the oil in a wok, add the chicken and stir-fry until browned.	2	Add the garlic, chili, and bell pepper and stir-fry until the pepper is soft.
3	Stir in the scallions, palm sugar, chili jam, and fish sauce and stir-fry until the sauce is thick and glossy.	4	Remove from the heat, add the basil leaves, and serve immediately with freshly cooked rice.

CHICKEN WITH LEMONGRASS

⤙ SERVES 4 • PREPARATION: 15 MINUTES • COOKING: 25 MINUTES ⤚

5 lemongrass stalks, chopped
2 large red chiles, deseeded and chopped
2 tablespoons vegetable oil

1½ lb chicken thigh fillets, cut into
bite-sized pieces
1 tablespoon shredded palm sugar

3 tablespoons fish sauce
freshly cooked rice, to serve

|---|---|---|---|
| 1 | Pound the lemongrass and chiles using a mortar and pestle or process in a food-mixer to form a rough paste. | 2 | Heat the oil in a wok, add the paste, and cook over a medium heat for 3 minutes, or until fragrant. |
| 3 | Add the chicken and stir-fry for 5 minutes, or until browned. Add the sugar and fish sauce and stir until the sugar begins to caramelize. | 4 | Serve with freshly cooked rice. |

CHICKEN WITH CASHEWS

❖ **SERVES 4** • PREPARATION: 15 MINUTES + 30 MINUTES MARINATING • COOKING: 15 MINUTES ❖

2 tablespoons cornstarch
1 lb chicken breast fillets, thinly sliced
2 tablespoons Shaoxing rice wine
2 tablespoons oyster sauce

1 tablespoon vegetable oil
1 onion, cut in half and thinly sliced
2 garlic cloves, chopped
1 carrot, thinly sliced

7 oz snow peas
7 oz cashews, toasted

1
4
2
5
3
6

1	Combine the cornstarch, chicken, rice wine, and oyster sauce.	2	Mix the chicken until it is coated in the marinade and marinate for 30 minutes.	3	Remove the chicken from the marinade. Heat the oil and brown the chicken.
4	Remove the chicken, add the onion and garlic, and fry for 3 minutes. Add the vegetables and fry briefly.	5	Return the chicken to the wok with ½ cup water and cook, stirring, until thick.	6	Add the cashews and serve.

TERIYAKI CHICKEN

⇾ SERVES 4 • PREPARATION: 5 MINUTES • COOKING: 25 MINUTES ⇽

8 chicken drumsticks
2 tablespoons vegetable oil
scant ½ cup sake
scant ½ cup mirin

scant ½ cup dark soy sauce
2 teaspoons superfine sugar
freshly cooked rice and vegetables, to serve

NOTE: You can cook any cut of chicken, meat, or tofu in this way.

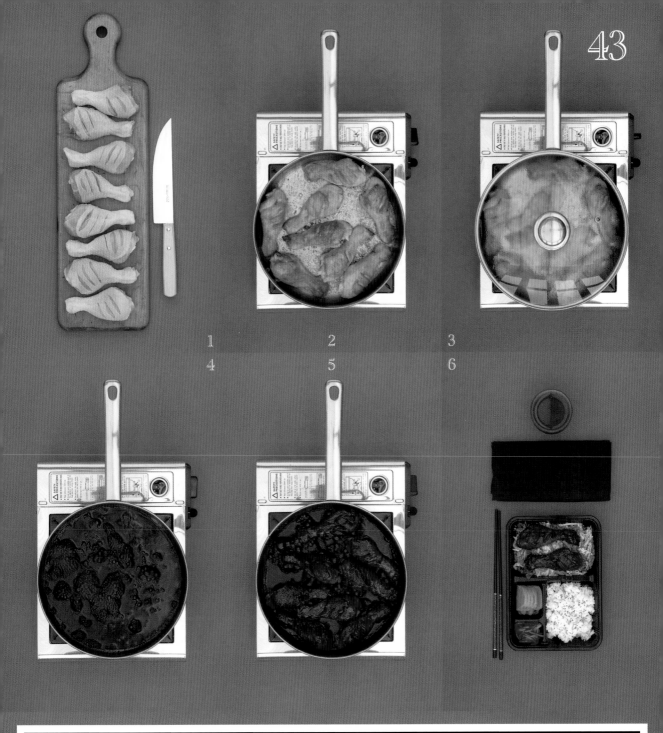

1	Score the chicken legs—this will help them cook evenly.	2	Heat the oil in a skillet, add the chicken, and cook for 10 minutes until browned.	3	Cover and cook for another 10 minutes. Remove the chicken from the skillet.
4	Add the sake, mirin, soy sauce, and sugar and boil until the sauce is glossy.	5	Return the chicken to the skillet and cook until caramelized in the sauce.	6	Serve the chicken with rice, vegetables, and any extra sauce.

VIETNAMESE CHICKEN SALAD

SERVES 4 • PREPARATION: 15 MINUTES + 30 MINUTES MARINATING • COOKING: 20 MINUTES

½ cup rice vinegar
2 tablespoons superfine sugar
1 red onion, thinly sliced

sea salt and black pepper
2 chicken breast fillets
8 oz Chinese cabbage, shredded

1 carrot, julienned
1 cup fresh Vietnamese mint
½ cup finely chopped, fried Asian shallots

1   2   3

4   5   6

1	Mix the vinegar and sugar together, add the onion, season with salt and pepper, and leave for 30 minutes.	2	Put the chicken in a skillet, add enough water to just cover, and cook gently for 15–20 minutes.	3	Remove the chicken and let cool before shredding.
4	Put the cabbage, carrot, mint, and chicken in a small bowl.	5	Add the onion and vinegar mixture and toss well to combine.	6	Serve topped with fried Asian shallots.

YAKITORI CHICKEN

❖ **SERVES 4** • PREPARATION: 20 MINUTES + 15 MINUTES SOAKING • COOKING: 20 MINUTES ❖

scant ½ cup sake
½ cup light soy sauce
3 tablespoons mirin

2 tablespoons superfine sugar
2 lb chicken thigh fillets
8 scallions

1
4

2
5

3
6

1	Soak several bamboo skewers in cold water for 15 minutes.	2	Bring the sake, soy, mirin, and sugar to a boil and cook for 5 minutes. Cool.	3	Cut the chicken into thick strips. Cut the spring onions into 2-inch pieces.
4	Thread the chicken and the spring onions onto the presoaked skewers.	5	Chargrill the chicken until tender, dipping the skewers in the sauce a couple of times during cooking.	6	Serve the chicken with the remaining sauce.

PEKING DUCK

❧ **SERVES 4–6** • PREPARATION: 15 MINUTES • COOKING: 5 MINUTES ❧

6 scallions
1 roast, glazed duck (see tip)
12 scallion pancakes

½ cup hoisin sauce
½ cucumber, cut into batons

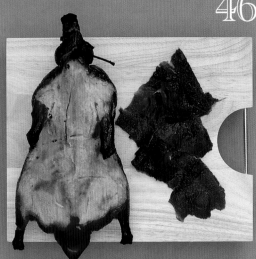

1 2
3 4

1	Cut the top of the scallions into thin strips without cutting all the way through and stand in a glass of ice water.	2	Using a sharp knife, slice the skin from the duck.
3	Put the pancakes in a bamboo steamer, cover, and steam over a wok of simmering water.	4	Place the pancakes in front of each guest and let them spoon a little hoisin sauce into the center of the pancakes. ➤

5	Top with some duck skin, a piece of spring onion, and cucumber.	**TIP** ❈ The pancakes can be found in the freezer section of Asian food stores.
TIP ❈ Purchase your duck from Chinatown or an Asian food store.		**SERVING SUGGESTION** ❈ To get the duck skin crisp, reheat it in an oven preheated to 425°F for 20 minutes. When it is cool enough to handle carefully remove the skin.

6	Roll up and eat immediately.	**TIP** ❄
		The duck carcass can be boiled in hot water to make a delicious bouillon.

TIP ❄	**TIP** ❄
Use the chopped leftover duck meat to make Sung Choi Bau (see recipe 20).	Use your homemade bouillon for soup or risotto.

MARINATED CHICKEN WINGS

❖ **SERVES 6** • PREPARATION: 20 MINUTES + 4–8 HOURS MARINATING • COOKING: 40 MINUTES ❖

2 lb chicken wings
1 teaspoon sesame oil
3 tablespoons soy sauce

2 tablespoons sweet chili sauce
2 tablespoons kecap manis
1 tablespoon lemon juice

1 2
3 4

1	Use a cleaver to remove the tips from the chicken wings.	2	Cut the wings through the center joint.	
3	Put the sesame oil, soy sauce, sweet chili sauce, kecap manis, and lemon juice in a bowl and mix to combine.	4	Add the chicken and toss to coat in the marinade. Cover and set aside in the fridge for at least 4 hours, or overnight.	➤

5 | Preheat the oven to 425°F. Arrange the chicken in a baking dish and cook for 40 minutes, turning midway during the cooking process.

VARIATION

❄

You can use chicken drumsticks instead of wings, if you prefer, and cook in the oven for 50 minutes.

6 Cook the wings until tender and sticky.

※

These chicken wings are also great served cold for picnics or in children's lunchboxes.

CRISPY SPICED DUCK

❧ SERVES 4 • PREPARATION: 15 MINUTES • COOKING: 30 MINUTES ❧

4 duck breasts, skin on
2 tablespoons all-purpose flour
½ teaspoon five-spice powder
½ teaspoon chili powder

1 teaspoon sea salt
peanut oil, for deep-frying
3 scallions, sliced
sprouting broccoli, to serve

PLUM SAUCE:
1 cup plum sauce
1–2 tablespoons rice vinegar

1 2
3 4

1	Put the duck breasts on a plate skin-side up and prick the skins of the duck using a skewer.	2	Put the plate in a large steamer over simmering water, cover, and cook for 10–15 minutes, or until the duck is cooked to medium.
3	Remove the duck and set aside on a wire rack until cool enough to handle.	4	Put the flour, five-spice powder, chili powder, and salt in a small bowl and mix to combine. ➤

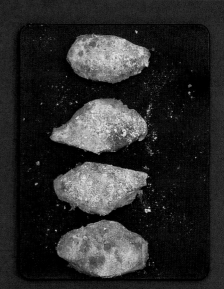

5	Coat the duck on both sides with the spiced flour mixture.	6	Shake off any excess flour.
7	Heat the oil and deep-fry the duck breasts for 3 minutes, or until the skin is crisp and golden. Cut into thin slices.	8	Heat the plum sauce and rice vinegar together until boiling.

9   Arrange the duck slices on a plate, garnish with scallions, and serve with plum sauce and broccoli.

TIP
❋

You can use salmon fillets instead of the duck. Make sure you buy pieces with the skin on.

VARIATION
❋

You can use bottled sweet-and-sour sauce instead of the plum sauce, if you prefer.

NASI GORENG

❖ SERVES 4 • PREPARATION: 20 MINUTES • COOKING: 10 MINUTES ❖

1 tablespoon peanut oil
1 teaspoon sambal oelek
2 garlic cloves, crushed
8 oz skinless chicken thigh fillets, finely chopped

8 oz peeled green shrimp, finely chopped
3 scallions, sliced
4 cups cold cooked rice
1 tablespoon kecap manis

1 tablespoon gluten-free soy sauce (tamari)
4 eggs
2 tomatoes, sliced
½ cucumber, sliced

1 2
3 4

1	Heat the oil in a wok, add the sambal oelek, garlic, chicken, and shrimp, and stir-fry until the chicken is golden.	2	Add the scallions and rice and stir-fry for 5 minutes, or until the rice is heated through.
3	Combine the sauces, stir in, and cook until hot. Remove from the wok and cover. Fry the eggs one at a time in the wok.	4	To serve, top a mound of rice on each plate with a fried egg and garnish with the sliced tomatoes and cucumber.

SEAFOOD

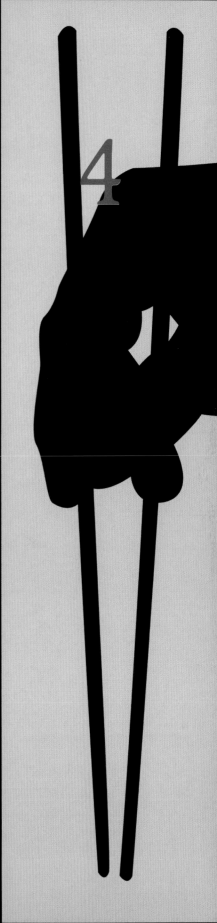

QUICK AND EASY DISHES

SIMPLE MAIN DISHES

RICE AND NOODLE DISHES

SUSHI

SWEET CHILI SQUID SALAD

➔ SERVES 4 • PREPARATION: 20 MINUTES • COOKING: 10 MINUTES ➔

1 lb cleaned baby squid, tentacles removed
1 tablespoon vegetable oil
3 tablespoons sweet chili sauce
1 tablespoon fish sauce

1 tablespoon lime juice
5 oz mixed salad leaves
2 oz bean sprouts
1 cucumber, thinly sliced

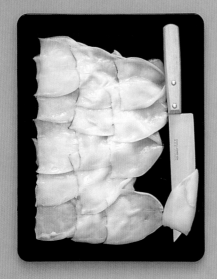

1 2
3 4

1	Cut the squid pouches in half and lay them skin-side down on a board.	2	Score the squid by cutting diagonally in one direction with the point of a knife, taking care not to cut all the way through.
3	Turn the board and cut in the other direction. Cut into small pieces.	4	Heat the oil in a wok until it starts to smoke. Add the squid and cook until it starts to curl up. ➤

5	Combine the sweet chili sauce, fish sauce, and lime juice and add to the wok. Cook until sticky.	**VARIATION** ❈ Use peeled shrimp instead of the squid.
	VARIATION ❈ Use ordinary squid instead of the baby squid.	**TIP** ❈ The squid in this sauce can be used for a stir-fry—add in some snow peas, broccoli, and asparagus.

6	Arrange the salad leaves on a platter, top with the bean sprouts and cucumber, and finish with the squid.	**TIP** ❈
		To save time, slice the squid pouches into rings.
SERVING SUGGESTION ❈		**SERVING SUGGESTION** ❈
This can be cooked on the grill on a flat plate. You might want to double the sauce ingredients.		This is a great dish to serve in small Chinese take-out boxes at a party.

ASIAN OYSTERS

➤ MAKES 24 • PREPARATION: 15 MINUTES • COOKING: 2 MINUTES ◄

2 lup cheong (Chinese sausages)
24 shucked oysters
1 tablespoon Worcestershire sauce
1 tablespoon shredded palm sugar

1 tablespoon fish sauce
1 tablespoon lime juice
1 large red chili, deseeded and
finely chopped

1 2
3 4

1	Finely chop the lup cheong sausage.	2	Arrange 12 of the oysters on a board. Put the remaining oysters onto a baking tray. Top with the Worcestershire sauce and lup cheong.	
3	Mix together the sugar, fish sauce, lime juice, and chili.	4	Divide the dressing among the raw oysters on the board.	➤

5	Broil the 12 oysters on the baking tray under a preheated broiler on high for 2 minutes, or until the sausage is crisp.

SERVING SUGGESTION
※

This topping also works well on halved mussels or you can serve a combination of the two.

VARIATION
※

Use bacon instead of the lup cheong sausage.

6	Serve the cooked hot oysters and raw cold oysters immediately.

❃

Serve the raw oysters drizzled with a little chili oil, some light soy sauce, chopped scallions, and shredded gingerroot.

VARIATION
❃

Try steaming the oysters then serve immediately with the dressing.

MUSSELS WITH LEMONGRASS

❧ **SERVES 4** • PREPARATION: 15 MINUTES • COOKING: 10 MINUTES ❧

2 lb live mussels
2 tablespoons vegetable oil
3 lemongrass stalks, thinly sliced
2 tablespoons finely shredded gingerroot

½ cup fish bouillon
1 tablespoon fish sauce
1 large red chili, deseeded and thinly sliced
½ cup fresh cilantro sprigs

3 scallions, sliced
juice from 1–2 limes

1	Scrub and debeard the mussels, discarding any that are open.	2	Heat the oil in a wok, add the lemongrass and ginger and cook for 2 minutes.	3	Add the mussels and toss to coat them in the lemongrass mixture.
4	Mix the bouillon and fish sauce together, then pour into the wok.	5	Cover and cook until the mussels open. Discard any that do not open.	6	Transfer the mussels to a bowl and top with the remaining ingredients.

SALT & PEPPER SQUID

➤ **SERVES 4–6** • PREPARATION: 30 MINUTES • COOKING TIME 10 MINUTES ➤

2 lb baby squid
4 tablespoons sea salt
3 tablespoons white peppercorns
2 teaspoons superfine sugar

1 cup cornstarch
1 cup all-purpose flour
4 egg whites, lightly beaten
peanut oil, for deep-frying

TO SERVE:
lemon wedges
soy sauce

1	Clean the squid. Cut the pouches into rings and the tentacles in half.	2	Grind the salt, peppercorns, and sugar using a mortar and pestle until they form a fine powder.	3	Transfer to a bowl, add the cornstarch and flour, and mix to combine.
4	Coat the squid in the egg whites, then toss in the seasoned flour until coated.	5	Heat the oil in a wok and fry the squid for 2 minutes, or until crisp. Drain.	6	Serve the squid with lemon wedges and soy sauce.

SEAFOOD RED CURRY

❧ SERVES 4 • PREPARATION: 10 MINUTES • COOKING: 25 MINUTES ❧

4 oz can bamboo shoots, rinsed and drained
1 lb raw jumbo shrimp
8 oz boneless white fish fillets
7 oz fresh scallops
2 tablespoons vegetable oil

2–3 tablespoons Thai red curry paste
2 teaspoons shrimp paste (optional)
2 cups coconut milk
1 tablespoon fish sauce
1 tablespoon shredded palm sugar

4 kaffir lime leaves, finely shredded
7 oz green beans, trimmed
steamed jasmine rice, to serve

1 2
3 4

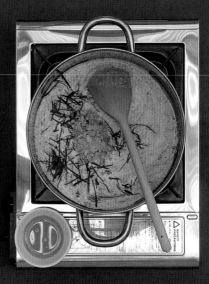

1	Cut the bamboo shoots into thin strips.	2	Peel and devein the shrimp, cut the fish into bite-sized pieces, and pat the scallops dry with paper towels.
3	Heat the oil in a pan, add the curry paste and shrimp paste, if using, and cook over a medium heat until the oil separates from the curry paste.	4	Add the coconut milk, fish sauce, sugar, and lime leaves, bring to a boil, then reduce the heat and cook for 10 minutes. ➢

5

Add the bamboo shoots and beans and cook for 5 minutes. Add the seafood and cook for a further 5 minutes, or until the fish is tender.

VARIATION
❀

Use a combination of seafood for this recipe or just use one type, if you prefer.

TIP
❀

If you are cooking this curry ahead of time, do not add the seafood until you are ready to serve; this way the fish will not break up.

| 6 | Serve with steamed jasmine rice. | |

STEAMED FISH WITH GINGER

❧ SERVES 4 • PREPARATION: 10 MINUTES • COOKING: 20 MINUTES ❧

4-inch piece fresh gingerroot
1½ lb boneless white fish fillets, such as
red snapper, sea bass, or cod
3 tablespoons Shaoxing rice wine

3 tablespoons light soy sauce
1 tablespoon superfine sugar
2 tablespoons peanut oil
1 teaspoon sesame oil

2 scallions, finely sliced
a few fresh cilantro sprigs
freshly steamed bok choi, to serve

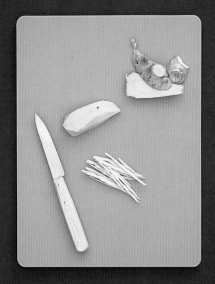

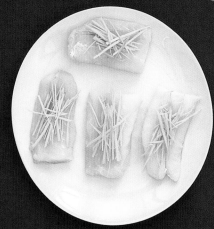

1 2
3 4

1	Peel and finely shred the gingerroot.	2	Put the fish on a large plate and sprinkle with the gingerroot.	
3	Put the rice wine, soy sauce, and sugar in a bowl and mix to combine.	4	Pour the rice wine mixture over the fish. Heat the oils in a pan until smoking, then pour over the fish.	➤

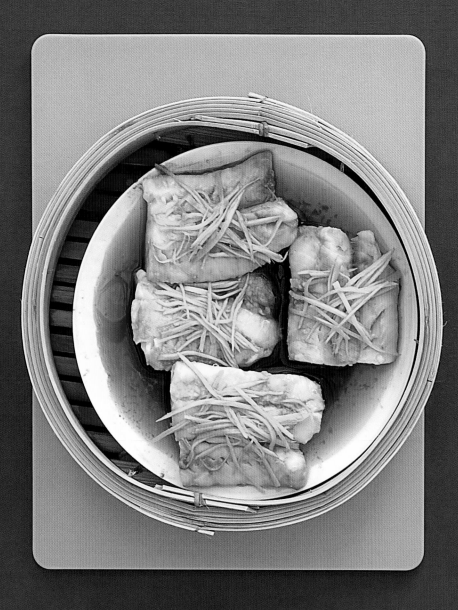

5	Put into a steamer over simmering water, then cover and steam for 15–20 minutes, or until the fish flakes easily.	**TIP** ❄ If you are watching your weight, you can simply steam the fish and serve with the dressing.
VARIATION ❄ Try steaming fresh shrimp or scallops and serving them with this dressing.		**SERVING SUGGESTION** ❄ You can cook Asian green vegetables in a steamer on top at the same time to serve with the fish.

6 Top with the scallions and cilantro and serve with bok choi.

VARIATION
❋

Substitute chicken for the fish if you prefer.

TIP
❋

You will need a large bamboo steamer for this recipe. Alternatively, use a smaller layered steamer and cook the fish fillets on individual plates.

SCALLOPS & SNOW PEAS

❧ SERVES 4 • PREPARATION: 10 MINUTES • COOKING: 10 MINUTES ❧

1 tablespoon vegetable oil
2 garlic cloves, chopped
1 tablespoon shredded fresh gingerroot
2 scallions, sliced

10 oz fresh scallops
7 oz snow peas
2 tablespoons Shaoxing rice wine
1 tablespoon light soy sauce

3 tablespoons chicken bouillon
freshly cooked rice, to serve

1 2
3 4

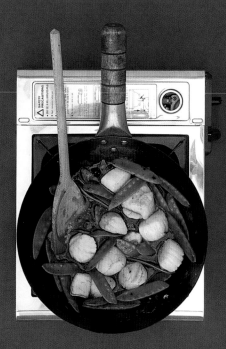

1	Heat the oil in a wok, add the garlic, ginger-root, and scallions and stir-fry for 2 minutes.	2	Add the scallops and snow peas and stir-fry for 3 minutes, or until the scallops turn white.
3	Mix the rice wine, soy sauce, and bouillon together. Add to the wok and cook until heated through.	4	Serve the scallops with freshly cooked rice.

CLAY POT SALMON

❧ **SERVES 2** • PREPARATION: 10 MINUTES • COOKING: 20 MINUTES ☙

1 tablespoon vegetable oil
2 salmon fillets, weighing about 7 oz each
4 tablespoons light brown sugar

4 tablespoons fish sauce
2 scallions, thinly sliced
freshly cooked rice, to serve

1 2
3 4

1	Heat the oil in a skillet until smoking, add the salmon, and cook until the skin is crisp. Remove and transfer to a clay pot or casserole.	2	Add the sugar and fish sauce to the pot and cook over a low heat until the sugar has completely dissolved.
3	Pour the caramel sauce into the clay pot, cover, and simmer for 15 minutes, or until the salmon is cooked to your liking.	4	Serve sprinkled with scallions and accompanied by freshly cooked rice. Note: You can also cook this in a skillet with a lid or a Dutch oven.

FISH WITH MISO

❧ **SERVES 4** • PREPARATION: 10 MINUTES + 10 MINUTES SOAKING • COOKING: 20 MINUTES ❧

4 dry Chinese mushrooms
7 oz soba noodles
2 tablespoons butter
2 tablespoons sake

2 tablespoons mirin
1 tablespoon soy sauce
1 tablespoon superfine sugar
3 tablespoons yellow miso

4 pieces boneless firm white fish fillets,
such as snapper or cod
2 scallions, thinly sliced
freshly cooked rice, to serve

1 2
3 4

1	Preheat the oven to 425°F. Soak the mushrooms in hot water for 10 minutes. Drain and finely shred the caps.	2	Cook the noodles in boiling water until just tender, then drain well.	
3	Put the butter, sake, mirin, soy sauce, and sugar into a pan and bring to a boil. Remove from the heat and stir in the miso.	4	Cut 4 squares of aluminum foil and put a mound of noodles in the center. Top with the fish, onions and mushrooms.	➤

5	Pour the sauce over the top and fold in the sides to enclose the parcel. Put on a nonstick baking tray and cook in the oven for 15 minutes, or until the fish is tender.

VARIATION
❈

Use chicken or tofu instead of the fish.

TIP
❈

Drain the mushrooms in step 1, then remove and discard the stalks before shredding the caps.

6	Serve the opened parcels on plates with freshly cooked rice.	**TIP** ❋ These parcels can also be cooked on the grill or under a hot broiler. **VARIATION** ❋ Substitute udon or hokkien noodles for the soba noodles, if you prefer.

SEAFOOD NOODLES

SERVES 4 • PREPARATION: 15 MINUTES • COOKING: 15 MINUTES

10 oz baby squid
10 oz raw shrimp
12 fresh scallops
1 tablespoon vegetable oil
1 teaspoon sesame oil

3 scallions, thinly sliced
1 tablespoon finely shredded gingerroot
1 red bell pepper, sliced
14 oz fresh hokkien noodles
2 tablespoons oyster sauce

2 tablespoons soy sauce
2 tablespoons kecap manis
1 bunch bok choi, finely chopped

1 2
3 4

1	Clean the squid and cut the pouch into rings. Cut the tentacles in half. Peel and devein the shrimp. Pat the scallops dry with paper towels.	2	Heat the oils in a wok over a high heat. Add the scallions, gingerroot, and bell pepper and cook for 3 minutes. Add the seafood and stir-fry over a high heat for 3 minutes, or until it changes color.
3	Add the noodles, oyster sauce, soy sauce, and kecap manis, then add the bok choi.	4	Stir-fry until the sauce is thick and glossy and the bok choi is wilted. Serve immediately.

FRIED RICE WITH SHRIMP

❧ SERVES 4 • PREPARATION: 15 MINUTES • COOKING: 15 MINUTES ❧

1 lb raw jumbo shrimp
3 tablespoons vegetable oil
3 eggs, lightly beaten

2 lup cheong (Chinese sausage) or 2 bacon
slices, chopped
1 tablespoon shredded fresh gingerroot
4 cups cooked and cooled white rice

2 tablespoons Shaoxing rice wine
2 tablespoons soy sauce
3 scallions, sliced

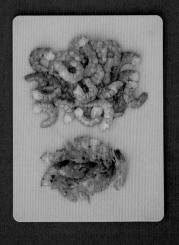

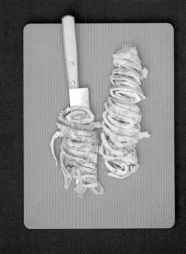

1
4

2
5

3
6

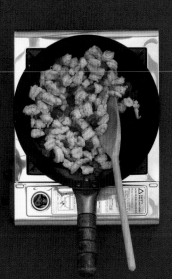

1	Peel and devein the shrimp and roughly chop.	2	Heat half the oil in a wok, add the eggs, and swirl to coat the base of the pan. Cook until set.	3	Remove the omelet from the wok, roll up, and cut into thin shreds.
4	Heat the remaining oil, add the shrimp, lup cheong, and ginger, and stir-fry briefly.	5	Add the rice, rice wine, and soy sauce and stir until heated through.	6	Add the scallions and toss until combined and hot. Serve immediately.

CHIRASHI SUSHI

✤ SERVES 4 • PREPARATION: 20 MINUTES • COOKING: 20 MINUTES ✦

1 tablespoon vegetable oil
2 eggs, lightly beaten
4 cups prepared Sushi Rice (see recipe 03)

1 sheet nori (seaweed), finely shredded
7 oz sashimi-grade salmon, thinly sliced
7 oz sashimi-grade tuna, thinly sliced

½ cucumber, sliced
½ teaspoon wasabi
3½ oz pickled ginger

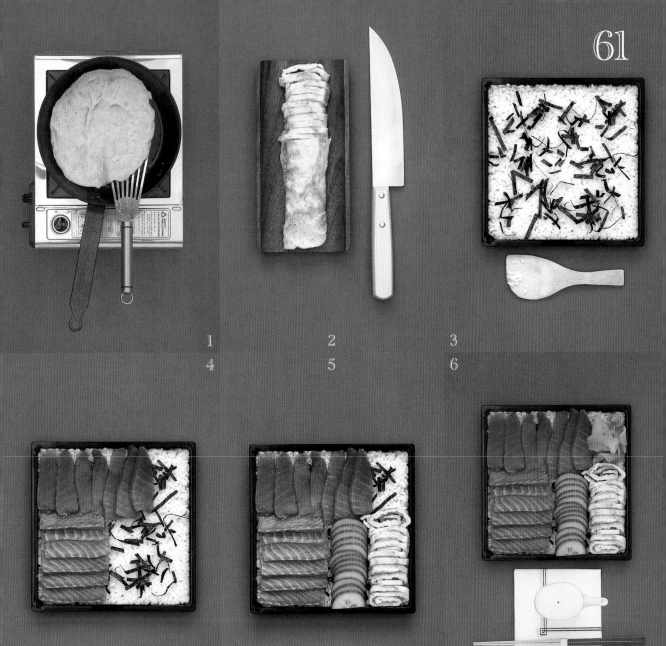

1	Heat the oil in a skillet, add the beaten eggs, and cook until set. Turn over and cook the other side.	2	Remove the omelet from the pan, let cool slightly, then roll up and cut into thin shreds.	3	Arrange the rice in 4 shallow lacquered boxes or plastic trays and scatter over the nori.
4	Arrange the salmon and tuna over the rice.	5	Arrange the cucumber and egg over the rice.	6	Put a squeeze of wasabi in the corner along with some pickled ginger and serve.

TEMAKI SUSHI

↠ SERVES 4 • PREPARATION: 15 MINUTES • COOKING: NIL IF YOU HAVE PREPARED THE RICE ↞

10 oz skinless salmon fillet
½ cucumber
1 avocado

4 sheets roasted nori (seaweed)
2 cups seasoned Sushi Rice
(see recipe 03)

¼ teaspoon wasabi, plus extra to serve
(optional)
soy sauce, to serve (optional)

1 2
3 4

1	Cut the salmon into thin strips with a sharp knife. Cut the cucumber and avocado into thin strips the same size as the salmon.	2	Cut the nori sheets into half and half again.
3	Put a tablespoon of cooked rice onto the center of each piece of nori. Top with a little wasabi, salmon, cucumber, and avocado strips.	4	Roll the nori over to form a cone shape and serve with soy sauce and extra wasabi, if you like.

VEGETABLES

DEEP-FRIED

CURRIES

EGGS

SIDE DISHES

AGEDASHI TOFU

❖ **SERVES 4** • PREPARATION TIME: 15 MINUTES + 15 MINUTES DRAINING • COOKING: 10 MINUTES ❖

1 lb silken firm tofu
all-purpose flour, for dusting
1 teaspoon dashi granules

2 tablespoons light soy sauce
2 tablespoons mirin
peanut oil, for deep-frying

TO SERVE:
2 tablespoons bonito flakes
2 scallions, finely shredded
freshly cooked rice

1 2 3
4 5 6

1	Put the tofu on paper towels on a board. Cover with paper towels and another board. Leave for 15 minutes.	2	Cut the tofu into ½-inch thick rectangles and pat dry with paper towel.	3	Lightly coat both sides of the tofu with the flour, shaking off any excess.
4	Cook the dashi in 2 cups boiling water with the soy and mirin for 5 minutes.	5	Heat the oil and cook the tofu until crisp and golden. Drain on paper towels.	6	Serve the tofu with the broth, bonito flakes, scallions, and rice.

VEGETABLE TEMPURA

❧ SERVES 4 • PREPARATION: 15 MINUTES • COOKING: 15 MINUTES ❧

DIPPING SAUCE:
⅛ teaspoon dashi granules
2 tablespoons mirin
2 tablespoons light soy sauce

TEMPURA BATTER:
2 egg yolks
2 cups chilled water
2 cups all-purpose flour
7 oz sweet potato, julienned

1 onion
1 red bell pepper, thinly sliced
3½ oz shiitake mushrooms
3½ oz green beans, trimmed
vegetable oil, for deep-frying

1 2
3 4

1	For the sauce, put the dashi, 2 tablespoons of water, mirin, and soy sauce in a pan and heat until boiling. Cool to room temperature.	2	For the batter, whisk the egg yolks and the chilled water together in a bowl. Sift in the flour and stir until just combined.
3	Put the sweet potato and onion in a bowl. Add half the tempura batter and roughly mix.	4	Dip the remaining vegetables in the batter, allowing any excess to drain off. ➤

5	Divide the sweet potato mixture into ¼ cup portions. Heat the oil and deep-fry the sweet potato mixture until crisp and golden. Drain on paper towels.	**TIP** ❁ To make a very light batter use chilled soda water instead of the water. **VARIATION** ❁ Use any vegetables for the tempura, such as baby spinach leaves, snow peas, and baby corn.	

| 6 | Cook the vegetables in the hot oil until crisp and golden. Serve the tempura on a plate with the dipping sauce on the side. | **TIP** ✤
It is best to deep-fry the tempura in batches and to drain on paper towels before serving.

SERVING SUGGESTION ✤
Double the dipping sauce ingredients and keep chilled to serve as a dressing for chilled soba noodles. |

VEGETABLE GREEN CURRY

❧ **SERVES 4** • PREPARATION: 15 MINUTES • COOKING: 30 MINUTES ❧

1 tablespoon vegetable oil
2 tablespoons green curry paste
7 oz firm tofu, cut into cubes
2 cups coconut milk

4 kaffir lime leaves, finely shredded
1 red bell pepper, sliced
2 zucchini, sliced
3½ oz baby corn

7 oz white mushrooms, halved
1 tablespoon shredded palm sugar
1 tablespoon lime juice
freshly cooked rice, to serve

1 2
3 4

Heat the oil in a pan, add the curry paste, and cook until the oil comes away from the paste.	2	Add the tofu and cook until browned.
Add the coconut milk, lime leaves, and vegetables and cook for 20 minutes, or until the vegetables are tender.	4	Season with palm sugar and lime juice and serve with freshly cooked rice.

SATAY PUMPKIN CURRY

✦ **SERVES 4** • PREPARATION: 15 MINUTES • COOKING: 30 MINUTES ✦

1 tablespoon vegetable oil
2 tablespoons satay paste
2 tablespoons shredded fresh gingerroot
1 lb pumpkin, peeled and cut into chunks

7 oz firm tofu, drained and cut into cubes
7 oz tomatoes
2 cups coconut cream
3½ oz baby spinach leaves

2 tablespoons chopped fresh cilantro
freshly cooked rice, to serve

1 2
3 4

1	Heat the oil in a pan, add the satay paste and ginger, and cook over a medium heat for 3 minutes, or until the oil starts to separate from the satay paste.	2	Add the pumpkin and cook until it is coated in the paste and softened slightly.
3	Add the tofu, tomatoes, and coconut cream. Bring to a boil, then lower the heat and cook for 20 minutes until the pumpkin is tender.	4	Stir in the spinach and cilantro and serve with freshly cooked rice.

CHINESE VEGETABLE OMELET

✦ SERVES 2 • PREPARATION: 15 MINUTES • COOKING: 10 MINUTES ✦

6 eggs
3 scallions, sliced
1 tablespoon light soy sauce

2 tablespoons vegetable oil
3½ oz shiitake mushrooms, sliced
1 tomato, chopped

½ bunch bok choi, roughly chopped
1¾ oz bean sprouts
1 tablespoon kecap manis

1 2
3 4

1	Beat the eggs, scallions, and soy sauce together.	2	Heat half the oil in a wok, add the mushrooms, and stir-fry for 5 minutes, or until browned. Remove from the wok.	
3	Heat the remaining oil in the wok, add the egg mixture, and swirl to cover the base of the wok.	4	Cook until nearly set, then add the mushrooms, tomato, bok choi, and bean sprouts.	➢

5	Fold the omelet in half to enclose the filling.	**VARIATION** ❀	
		These omelets are also delicious filled with fried rice.	
TIP ❀		**VARIATION** ❀	
You can make smaller individual omelets rather than a large one, if you prefer.		Use any vegetable for the filling and add some fried tofu or some cooked egg noodles.	

6	Fold the omelet in half again and remove from the wok. Drizzle with kecap manis and serve.	**SERVING SUGGESTION** ❈ These omelets can be served for breakfast, lunch, or as an easy dinner.
VARIATION ❈ Use oyster sauce instead of kecap manis, if you prefer.		**TIP** ❈ Make sure the oil is hot before adding the egg mixture in step 3.

GADO GADO

➤ SERVES 4 • PREPARATION: 20 MINUTES • COOKING: 10 MINUTES ⬧

5 oz cabbage, shredded
7 oz green beans, trimmed
2 carrots, sliced
2 potatoes, sliced
3½ oz bean sprouts

2 hard-cooked eggs, peeled and quartered
2 tablespoons fried Asian shallots
PEANUT SAUCE:
¼ cup peanut oil
7 oz peanuts

2 garlic cloves, chopped
4 shallots, chopped
½ teaspoon sambal oelek
1 tablespoon kecap manis
1 tablespoon tamarind concentrate (paste)

1 2
3 4

1	Steam or boil all the vegetables apart from the fried Asian shallots until tender.	2	For the sauce, heat the oil in a wok and fry the peanuts until golden. Remove with a slotted spoon and drain. Set aside 1 tablespoon of oil.	
3	Put the peanuts into a food-mixer and process into a powder. Remove. Pound the garlic and shallots to a paste with a pestle and mortar.	4	Heat the reserved oil in the wok, add the garlic–shallot mixture and cook until golden.	➤

5	Add the peanuts, sambal oelek, kecap manis, tamarind concentrate, and 2 cups of water. Cook, stirring occasionally, until the sauce boils and thickens.	**VARIATION** ❀
		Use any vegetables for this recipe—try snow peas, cauliflower, sweet potato, and broccoli.
		SERVING SUGGESTION ❀
		This is a great salad to make ahead of time and serve at barbecues.

6	Serve the vegetables and egg with the peanut sauce and fried Asian shallots.	**SERVING SUGGESTION** ✽ You can also serve some fried tempeh or tofu with the sauce.
TIP ✽		**SERVING SUGGESTION** ✽
This recipe makes quite a lot of peanut sauce, so store in an airtight container in the fridge and serve with grilled chicken wings.		Serve the gado gado with fried cassava chips, which are available from Asian food stores.

PICKLED VEGETABLE SALAD

➤ MAKES 4 CUPS • PREPARATION: 50 MINUTES + 8 HOURS PICKLING • COOKING: NIL ◄

2 carrots
1 large daikon (white radish)
7 oz bean sprouts
1 cucumber

1 red chile
2 tablespoons sea salt
1 cup rice vinegar
½ cup water

2 tablespoons superfine sugar
3 tablespoon fresh mint leaves
3 tablespoons fresh Vietnamese
mint leaves

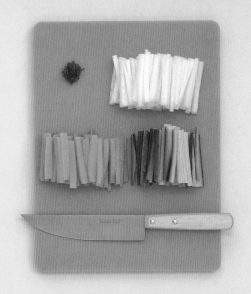

1 2
3 4

1	Peel and cut the vegetables into thick batons. Chop the chile finely.	2	Put the vegetables into a nonmetallic dish and sprinkle with the salt.	
3	Let stand for 30 minutes, then rinse thoroughly.	4	Pack the vegetables into a vacuum-sealed jar.	➤

5	Mix the water, rice vinegar, and sugar together and pour over the vegetables.	**TIP** ❈ Be sure to use a sterilized jar with an airtight lid.
TIP ❈ Most Vietnamese meals are served with some of these pickles on the side.		**VARIATION** ❈ You can vary the vegetables you use or cut the vegetables into decorative shapes.

		VARIATION
6	Seal and allow to stand overnight. Serve with mint and Vietnamese mint tossed through.	If you cannot find Vietnamese mint leaves, use ordinary mint instead.
TIP		**TIP**
Before chopping the red chili, remove the seeds, if you prefer.		Wash your hands thoroughly after preparing chiles as the volatile oils in them can cause irritation.

STEAMED TOFU WITH GINGER

❖ SERVES 4 • PREPARATION: 10 MINUTES • COOKING: 10 MINUTES ❖

1 lb silken firm tofu
1 tablespoon finely shredded fresh gingerroot
2 tablespoons Shaoxing rice wine

2 tablespoons light soy sauce
1 teaspoon superfine sugar
3 scallions, sliced
1 large red chile, deseeded and thinly sliced

2 tablespoons fried Asian shallots
½ teaspoon white pepper

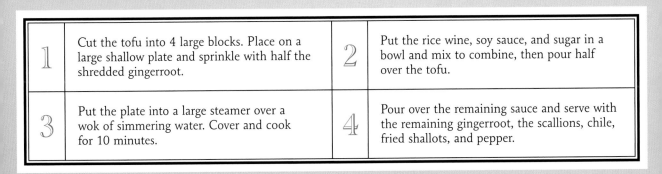

1	Cut the tofu into 4 large blocks. Place on a large shallow plate and sprinkle with half the shredded gingerroot.	2	Put the rice wine, soy sauce, and sugar in a bowl and mix to combine, then pour half over the tofu.
3	Put the plate into a large steamer over a wok of simmering water. Cover and cook for 10 minutes.	4	Pour over the remaining sauce and serve with the remaining gingerroot, the scallions, chile, fried shallots, and pepper.

NOODLES WITH VEGETABLES

❧ SERVES 4 • PREPARATION: 15 MINUTES • COOKING: 10 MINUTES ❧

8 oz dried egg noodles
1 tablespoon vegetable oil
1 teaspoon sesame oil
10 oz firm tofu, cut into strips

1 red bell pepper, sliced
1 carrot, sliced
1 zucchini, sliced
7 oz snow peas

7 oz broccoli, cut into florets
3 tablespoons kecap manis
2 teaspoons sambal oelek

1 2
3 4

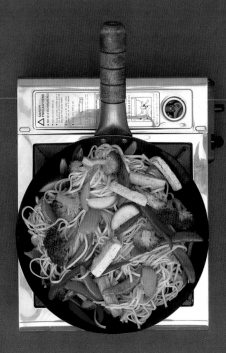

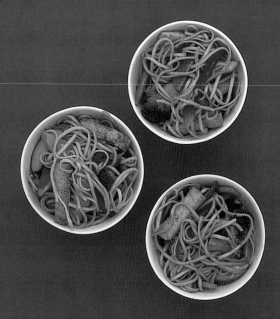

1	Cook the noodles in a pan of boiling water until just tender. Drain well.	2	Heat the oils in a wok, add the tofu, and stir-fry over a high heat until golden.
3	Add the vegetables and stir-fry for 3 minutes. Combine the kecap manis and sambal oelek. Add the noodles and kecap manis mixture to the wok and fry until the noodles are coated.	4	Divide the noodles and vegetables among 4 serving bowls and serve immediately.

SPINACH & BEAN SALAD

❧ **SERVES 4** • PREPARATION: 15 MINUTES + 15 MINUTES SOAKING • COOKING: 15 MINUTES ❧

⅓ oz wakame (seaweed)
7 oz green beans, trimmed
10 oz baby spinach

DRESSING
2 tablespoons sesame seeds, toasted
1 egg yolk
3 tablespoons white miso

2 tablespoons sake
½ tablespoon superfine sugar
1 tablespoon mirin

1	Soak the wakame (seaweed) in lukewarm water for 15 minutes. Drain well.	2	Steam the beans and spinach until tender, then rinse and cut in half.	3	For the dressing, lightly grind the sesame seeds with a mortar and pestle.
4	Transfer half the sesame seeds to a bowl, stir in the remaining ingredients, and beat to combine.	5	Put the wakame on a plate and top with the spinach and beans.	6	Drizzle with the dressing and serve sprinkled with the remaining sesame seeds on top.

STIR-FRIED MIXED VEGETABLES

➤ SERVES 4 • PREPARATION: 15 MINUTES • COOKING: 15 MINUTES ◄

1 tablespoon vegetable oil
1 onion, thinly sliced
2 garlic cloves, chopped
7 oz asparagus, cut into 2-inch pieces

7 oz sprouting broccoli, roughly chopped
7 oz snow peas
10 oz Chinese cabbage, roughly chopped
½ cup water

3 tablespoons Shaoxing rice wine
1 tablespoon light soy sauce
1 tablespoon cornstarch

1 2
3 4

1	Heat the oil in a wok, add the onion and garlic, and stir-fry for 3 minutes, or until the onion is soft.	2	Add the vegetables, stir-fry for 2 minutes, then add the water.
3	Mix together the rice wine, soy sauce, and cornstarch.	4	Add to the vegetables and cook, stirring, until the sauce boils and thickens. Serve.

ASIAN GREENS

❖ **SERVES 4** • PREPARATION: 5 MINUTES • COOKING: 8 MINUTES ❖

1 tablespoon sesame seeds
3 bunches bok choi
2 tablespoons oyster sauce
1 teaspoon sesame oil

1 2
3 4

1	Toast the sesame seeds in a wok until golden.	2	Wash the bok choi and cut into quarters.
3	Arrange the bok choi evenly over the base of a large steamer and steam in a wok over simmering water for 3–5 minutes until tender.	4	Drizzle with the oyster sauce and sesame oil, and sprinkle with the sesame seeds just before serving.

DESSERTS

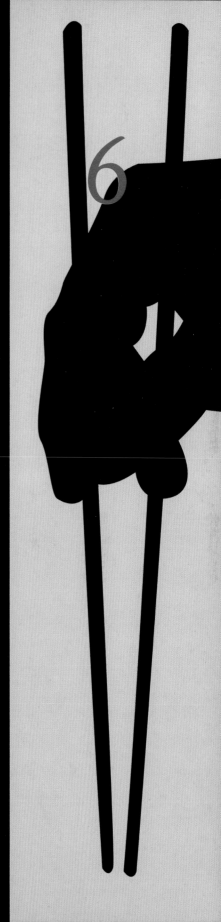

FRUIT DISHES

RICE DISHES

CREAM

WATERMELON & LITCHI ICE

SERVES 4–6 • PREPARATION: 20 MINUTES + 8 HOURS FREEZING • COOKING: 2 MINUTES

1 lb 4 oz can litchis in natural syrup
1 lb watermelon, deseeded and chopped
2 tablespoons shredded fresh gingerroot

⅓ cup superfine sugar
¼ cup lime juice

1 2
3 4

1	Drain the litchis, retaining 1 cup of the liquid.	2	Put the litchis and watermelon into a food-mixer and process until puréed.
3	Strain through a fine-mesh strainer, pressing down on any pulp with a back of a metal spoon to remove as much juice as possible. Discard the pulp.	4	Heat the reserved juice, gingerroot, sugar and lime juice until sugar dissolves, then bring to a boil. Let stand for 10 minutes. Strain, add to the purée, and let cool. ➤

5	Pour the mixture into a shallow metal baking pan or bowl and put in the freezer. Let the mixture start to form an icy edge, which takes about 2 hours. Using a fork, gently mix and mash the ice mixture. Do this every 1–2 hours until you get a nice slushy effect, then freeze completely. You may need to leave it overnight.	**VARIATION** ❈ Substitute mango for the watermelon and add some fresh mint or rose water to the recipe.

6	Serve the ice in small dishes.	SERVING SUGGESTION ✳
		This ice makes a delicious palate cleanser served between courses at a dinner party.

TIP ✳	VARIATION ✳
The larger the metal tray you use the quicker the liquid will freeze.	Add a little vodka or tequila, blend, and serve as a refreshing summer cocktail.

DEEP-FRIED BANANAS

⇝ SERVES 4 • COOKING: 15 MINUTES • PREPARATION: 15 MINUTES ⇜

2 cups all-purpose flour
¼ cup superfine sugar, plus extra for sprinkling
1 egg, lightly beaten

2 cups soda water
4 bananas
2 cups peanut oil
ice cream, to serve

1 2
3 4

1	Put the flour and sugar in a bowl and make a well in the center.	2	Mix then pour into the center of the bowl and mix to form a smooth batter.	
3	Cut the bananas in half lengthways then in half across the width.	4	Dip the bananas into the batter, allowing any excess to drain off.	➤

5	Heat the oil in a large wok and deep-fry the bananas until golden. Drain on paper towels.	**TIP** ❋
		If you don't have a large wok use a deep saucepan to deep-fry the bananas in step 5.

VARIATION ❋	**SERVING SUGGESTION** ❋
For a more spicy batter, add ½ teaspoon each of powdered cinnamon and cardamon to the batter.	For a typically Asian touch, add some toasted sesame seeds to the batter.

6	Sprinkle with sugar and serve with ice cream.	**VARIATION** ❋ Substitute thinly sliced apple for the bananas.
TIP ❋ Try to use ripe bananas and cook them just before serving so they are nice and crisp.		**SERVING SUGGESTION** ❋ Make a caramel sauce and pour this over the bananas at the end.

BLACK STICKY RICE

⇾ **SERVES 4** • PREPARATION: 10 MINUTES + 8 HOURS SOAKING • COOKING: 30 MINUTES ⇽

2 cups black glutinous rice
4 cups cold water
2 cups coconut milk
½ cup shredded palm sugar

TO SERVE:
½ cup coconut milk
fresh mango

1 2
3 4

1	Put the rice into a bowl, cover with cold water, and let stand overnight.	2	Bring the rice and the measured cold water to a boil, then lower the heat and simmer for 20 minutes. Drain well.
3	Put the coconut milk and sugar into another pan and stir until the sugar has dissolved. Add the rice and cook for 10 minutes until hot.	4	Cover and set aside until ready to serve. When ready, drizzle the coconut milk over the top and serve with half a mango per person.

STICKY RICE

❧ **SERVES 4** • PREPARATION: 5 MINUTES + 8 HOURS SOAKING • COOKING: 20 MINUTES ❧

2 cups white sticky rice
1 cup coconut milk
¼ cup white granulated sugar
fresh fruit of your choice, to serve

1
4

2
5

3
6

1	Soak the rice in a bowl of cold water overnight. Rinse and drain well.	2	Put the rice in a steamer lined with baking paper that is pierced with holes.	3	Put the steamer into a wok over simmering water, cover, and cook for 20 minutes.
4	Transfer the rice to a bowl, add the coconut milk and sugar, and mix well.	5	Cover and set aside until the rice has absorbed the coconut milk.	6	Serve the sticky rice with fruit of your choice.

CASHEW STAR ANISE BRÛLÉE

❧ **SERVES 6** • PREPARATION: 25 MINUTES + 4 HOURS CHILLING • COOKING: 30 MINUTES ❧

8 oz roasted unsalted cashew nuts
2 cups milk
3 cups heavy cream
3 star anise, broken and bruised

1 cup superfine sugar
6 egg yolks
¼ cup superfine sugar, to make the brûlée

1	Preheat the oven to 325°F. Put the cashew nuts in a food-mixer and whiz to form a smooth paste.	2	Heat the milk, cream, cashew paste, star anise, and ¾ cup of sugar to boiling point. Set aside for 10 minutes. Strain the cream mixture.
3	Beat the egg yolks and remaining sugar together in a bowl until thick and pale. Beat the infused milk into the egg mixture.	4	Divide the mixture among 6 individual ramekins and put into a water bath. ➤

5	Bake for 30 minutes, or until set. Let cool to room temperature, then chill for 4 hours. When ready to serve, sprinkle the tops with the ¼ cup superfine sugar and use a cook's blowtorch to caramelize the sugar.	**TIP** ✳
		If you don't have a blowtorch you can cook the brûlee under a very hot broiler until the sugar caramelizes.

6	Serve immediately.	**TIP** *❋* If you don't have 6 individual ramekin dishes, you can make one large crème brûlée instead. Make sure you add enough hot water to come midway up the sides of the dish in the water bath, and cook for 1 hour.

VARIATION
❋

Substitute almonds or pistachios for the cashew nuts, if you prefer.

LIME & GINGER TART

❧ **SERVES 6–8** • PREPARATION: 30 MINUTES + 20 MINUTES CHILLING • COOKING: 1¼ HOURS ❧

2 cups all-purpose flour
4 oz butter, chopped
2 tablespoons superfine sugar
1 egg, lightly beaten

FILLING:
2 eggs + 3 egg yolks
½ cup superfine sugar
¾ cup lime juice

2 tablespoons lime peel
3½ fl oz heavy cream
2 tablespoons chopped preserved stem ginger
½ cup lime or ginger preserve

1

2

3

4

5

6

| 1 | Preheat the oven to 350°F. Put the flour in a bowl and rub in the butter to make crumbs. | 2 | Stir in the sugar, egg, and 3–4 tablespoons chilled water until the mixture forms a soft dough. | 3 | Roll out the dough and use to fit a 9-inch tart pan. Prick the base with a fork. Chill for 20 minutes. |
| 4 | Blind bake the pie shell for 20 minutes. Uncover and bake for 10 minutes. | 5 | Combine all the filling ingredients, except for the preserve. | 6 | Pour into the case and bake (see tip) for 35–45 minutes. Cool. ➢ |

7	Put the preserve in a pan and stir over a low heat until it melts.

VARIATION

※

Use orange preserve on top instead of the lime or ginger preserve, if you prefer.

TIP

※

Before baking the filled tart (see step 6), be sure to reduce the oven temperature to 325°F.

8 | Pour the melted preserve over the top of the tart and let cool. Serve cut into wedges.

VARIATIONS
❋

For a stronger ginger flavor add 1 teaspoon of powdered gingerroot to the egg mixture and use candied ginger instead of preserved stem ginger.

SERVING SUGGESTION
❋

This tart is delicious served either warm or cold with sour cream or cream. Store in an airtight container in the fridge after slicing.

KAFFIR LIME CRÈME CARAMEL

❖ SERVES 4 • PREPARATION: 30 MINUTES + 4 HOURS CHILLING • COOKING: 50 MINUTES ❖

6 kaffir lime leaves
½ cup white granulated sugar
1 cup milk

1 cup coconut milk
½ cup superfine sugar
4 eggs, lightly beaten

1 2
3 4

1	Preheat the oven to 325°F. Shred the lime leaves finely.	2	Gently heat the granulated sugar in a pan until it dissolves. Increase the heat and cook until it caramelizes. Divide among 4 ramekins.	
3	Heat the milk, coconut milk, and shredded lime leaves until boiling point. Remove from the heat and leave for 15 minutes. Strain.	4	Beeat the superfine sugar and eggs together in a bowl to combine.	➤

| 5 | Add the milk and divide the mixture among the ramekins. Put the ramekins in a water bath and add enough water to come midway up the side of the dishes. Bake for 40 minutes, or until set. | **TIP**
❋
Make sure you let the desserts chill completely, preferably overnight, otherwise it may be difficult to get them out of the molds. |

6	Chill for 4 hours before inverting onto serving plates.	**TIP** ❋ Be sure to use 1-cup capacity ramekin dishes that are heatproof.
TIP ❋ If you like a stronger kaffir lime flavor, use all milk rather than coconut milk for this recipe.		**VARIATION** ❋ If you prefer, use an 8-inch diameter dish to make one large crème caramel, and cook for 1 hour.

SAGO PUDDING

❧ **SERVES 4** • PREPARATION: 5 MINUTES • COOKING: 20 MINUTES + 30 MINUTES STANDING ❧

½ cup sago
2 cups water
1¾ cups coconut cream
¼ cup shredded palm sugar

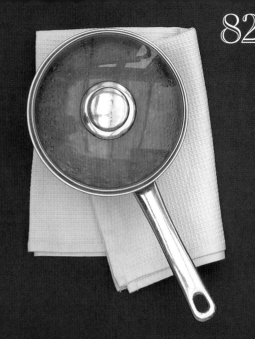

1 2
3 4

1	Put the sago and the measured water into a pan, bring to a boil, and cook over a high heat for 10 minutes.	2	Turn off the heat, cover, and let stand for 30 minutes, or until the sago becomes thick and transparent.
3	Add the coconut cream and palm sugar.	4	Stir over a medium heat for 10 minutes, or until the sago thickens. Serve immediately.

GREEN TEA PANNA COTTA

↠ **SERVES 6** • PREPARATION: 25 MINUTES + 4 HOURS CHILLING • COOKING: 5 MINUTES ↞

1 tablespoon Japanese green tea powder
1 cup milk
2 cups heavy cream

½ cup superfine sugar
1½ tablespoons powdered gelatin
vegetable oil, for oiling

1

2

3

4

5

6

1	Blend the green tea powder with a little of the milk to dissolve it, then gradually add the remaining milk.	2	Heat the tea, milk, cream, and sugar until the sugar dissolves, then heat to boiling point. Set aside.	3	Blend the gelatin with a little warm water until soft. Beat into the milk mixture until it dissolves.
4	Lightly oil 6 x ½-cup molds or ramekins.	5	Divide the mixture among the ramekins and chill for 4 hours, or until set.	6	Rub the outside of the molds with a damp cloth and invert onto plates.

APPENDICES

GLOSSARY

MENUS

TABLE OF CONTENTS

INDEX OF RECIPES

GENERAL INDEX

ACKNOWLEDGMENTS

GLOSSARY

ASIAN SHALLOTS
These are smaller than French shallots and come in small purplish bunches that resemble long garlic cloves. French shallots or red onions may be used as a substitute. Shallots are used in curry pastes, soups, and salads. You can deep-fry them and add them to salads, or use as a garnish. Deep-fried shallots can be purchased in jars in Asian food stores.

BAMBOO SHOOTS
The young cone-shaped shoots of the bamboo plant are usually sold in cans and have more flavor than their pre-sliced counterparts. Rinse under cold running water before using.

BLACK GLUTINOUS ("STICKY") RICE
Black sticky rice is only used to make desserts, and, like white sticky rice, it needs to be soaked in cold water overnight before cooking.

BONITO FLAKES
These are made from dried skipjack tuna and are much used in Japanese cooking. The bonito is shaved in fine slivers, which are sprinkled over dishes just before serving to add a mild fish flavor.

COCONUT MILK/CREAM
Coconut cream is thicker than coconut milk and will solidify at the top of the can. It is usually used to cook curry paste in instead of oil. If you want to use coconut cream, do not shake the can before opening—you can then remove the thick cream with a spoon. Alternatively, you can buy cartons of coconut cream in most big food stores. Use coconut milk in curries or stir-fries.

CHILES
Large red chiles—These are widely used in Thai cooking to add color. They are mild and can be tolerated by most palates if you remove the seeds.
Small red—Also known as bird's eye chiles, these are fiery. The heat is in the seed and membrane. For a spicy dish, chop the flesh and include the seeds; for a milder dish, halve the chile; and for a very mild dish leave them whole and discard before serving. Always protect your hands when preparing chiles.
Dried large red—These are not so spicy because the seeds have been removed. To use, soak them in hot water for 10 minutes, then drain and chop. Dried chiles are used to make red curry pastes.

Small green—These chiles are milder than small red chiles and can be used to make green curry paste. They are not as hot as large green chiles.
Large green—These chiles are hotter than large red chiles and can be used to make green curry paste if you would like it really spicy.

CHILI JAM
This is a thick sweet chili paste sold in Asian food stores. It is used in Thai cooking and is an essential ingredient in any dish that uses chile and basil.

CILANTRO
Also known as coriander or Chinese parsley, this is widely used in Thai and Chinese cooking. The root is often used in making curry pastes. Cilantro has a delicious peppery flavor. Store wrapped in damp paper towels in an airtight container or plastic bag.

DASHI
This is an essential ingredient in Japanese cooking and is known as basic bouillon. You can buy dashi granules and just add water to make bouillon or you can make your own by simmering dried bonito flakes and kelp in water before straining the liquid.

DRIED CHINESE (SHIITAKE) MUSHROOMS
These mushrooms vary in price and quality. To reconstitute, cover with boiling water and let stand for 10 minutes. Remove the stems and discard, then finely shred the caps. The soaking liquid may be used to add flavor to soups and sauces.

DRIED MUNG BEAN VERMICELLI
Also called glass noodles, these are clear thread-like noodles that are used in salads and spring rolls. Vermicelli need to be soaked in water before using.

DRIED RICE NOODLES
These long thin white noodles are best known for their use in Pad Thai. Soak them in cold water for 15 minutes; this way they will not overcook and break up when you add them to the wok.

DRIED SHRIMP
Tiny shrimp that have been dried in the sun, these are widely used in Asian cooking to add a mild shrimp flavor to dishes. They can be fried in oil or added as they are to salads or stir-fries.

FISH SAUCE

This is made from fermented, salted anchovies and is widely used in Thai and Vietnamese cooking instead of salt. The Thais call it nam pla and the Vietnamese nuoc man. Its level of saltiness will vary depending on the brand, so it is a good idea to taste before using.

FRESH RICE NOODLES

These flat rice noodles are available at ambient temperature in Asian food stores, and sold either pre-sliced or in blocks that need to be cut into strips before using. Avoid refrigerating them if you can, as this tends to make them break up. Try to buy them on the day you need them.

GALANGAL

This looks like a dark pink gnarled gingerroot but its flesh is firmer and woodier and its flavor is much more concentrated. To use, peel and pound. You can add slices to soups, but it is best known for its use in Tom Kai Gai. If you cannot find it, use gingerroot.

GINGERROOT

Fresh gingerroot is widely used in Asian cooking; its peppery flavor intensifies with age. Peel before using, then shred and add to stir-fries or curries, or cut into thin slices and add to soups or braises.

GREEN PAPAYA

This is an unripe papaya used in salads. To use, peel and remove the pits then shred finely.

GREEN TEA NOODLES

These are buckwheat noodles that have had green tea powder added.

GREEN TEA POWDER

This is used in Japanese desserts. Use it sparingly as it is quite expensive. It needs to be blended with a little milk or water before using.

GYOZA WRAPPERS

White square wheat flour wrappers used to make Japanese dumplings of the same name. They are found in the refrigerator section of Asian food stores.

HOISIN

Probably best known as the sauce served on Peking duck pancakes, hoisin sauce is made from salted yellow beans, sugar, vinegar, sesame oil, and five-spice powder. It is delicious on its own as a dipping sauce for Vietnamese rice paper rolls or when added to marinades and sauces.

JAPANESE CURRY

This paste-like curry is available in a variety of temperatures and is sold in boxes in Asian food stores. Purchase according to your palate.

JAPANESE MAYONNAISE

This thick squeezable mayonnaise is prized by the Japanese as a condiment and is also used as a sushi flavoring. It is sold in jars in Asian food stores. The flavor is much stronger than the western version of mayonnaise.

JASMINE RICE

This is a fragrant long-grain rice that is highly prized in Thai cooking. It is steamed and served at all meals. Rinse the rice thoroughly before using. Basmati rice has a totally different flavor and is not really considered to be a substitute.

KAFFIR LIME LEAVES

These are fragrant, glossy, double leaves that give Thai and Indonesian dishes their distinctive taste. To use, remove the tough middle stem, tear the leaves and add to soups and curries, or finely shred them in salads and stir-fries. Fresh leaves can be frozen. Dried leaves can be used, but they don't have the wonderful pungent lime flavor of fresh ones.

KECAP MANIS

This is a thick sweet soy sauce that is used in stir-fries, dipping sauces, dressings, and marinades. Indonesian kecap manis comes in three types: sweet (red label), mild sweet (yellow label), and salty (green label).

LEMONGRASS

A long strappy grass-like herb widely used in Thai and Vietnamese cooking. The firm white portion is finely chopped or pounded and used in curries, stir-fries, or marinades, while the grassy tops can be used in teas.

LUP CHEONG

This is a sweet Chinese sausage or salami.

MIRIN

This is a very sweet rice wine that is used only for cooking and not for drinking. It adds sweetness to dishes and gives broiled basted foods such as Yakitori a glossy finish. If you can't find mirin you can use sake sweetened with sugar instead. Add 1 teaspoon of sugar to 1 tablespoon of sake.

MISO

This is fermented soybean paste and is widely used in Japanese cuisine. As a rule, the lighter the color, the milder the flavor, and the darker the color, the richer and more salty the flavor. Light miso is more widely used in summer and dark miso is used in winter.

NORI

These are flat square sheets of seaweed that are used to make sushi. You can purchase nori roasted or unroasted, but the roasted sheets have more flavor.

OYSTER SAUCE

This sauce is widely used in Cantonese cuisine. It is a thick dark sauce made from oyster extract, sugar, salt, caramel, and flour and is used in stir-fries and marinades. Vegetarians can purchase mushroom oyster sauce, which is less thick.

PALM SUGAR

This is a type of sugar made from the sap of the trunk of the coconut or sugar palm. It is sold in round blocks and comes in two colors: blond or dark brown. Use a sharp knife to shave the firmer block or shred the softer ones. If you can't buy palm sugar, you can use light brown sugar instead.

PANKO BREAD CRUMBS

These are coarse-textured Japanese bread crumbs, which are an essential ingredient in Tonkatsu. They are sold in bags in Asian food stores. If you can't find them you can make your own by toasting and roughly crushing one-day-old bread.

PICKLED GINGER

This is sliced ginger that has been pickled in vinegar and often dyed to give a pink blush, though the flavor is the same in the uncolored version. Served with both sushi and sashimi, pickled ginger is used widely as a condiment in Japan.

RED CURRY PASTE

This is made from dried red chiles that have been pounded with Asian shallots and spices. It is not as hot as green curry paste, but it is a good idea to test for heat before adding to dishes as brands will vary. Asian brands are usually a little spicier.

RICE PAPER ROUNDS

These dried rice disks are used to make Vietnamese rice paper rolls. To use, soak in lukewarm water. They come in a variety of sizes; larger are easier to roll.

RICE VINEGAR

Chinese rice vinegar is made from fermented rice. It is available in a variety of colors and each color has its specific use. Clear vinegar is used for pickles and if you can't find it you can substitute cider vinegar instead. Red rice vinegar is used as a dipping sauce for dumplings and the black version is used in braises and broths.

SAGO

Small pearls of sago are made from the root of the cassava plant. Cooked in water until it becomes translucent it can then be flavored with coconut milk, mango, or other fruits. It is served either warm or cold as a dessert.

SAKE

This is rice wine that is widely used in Japanese cooking as a tenderizer. It moderates the saltiness of a dish and removes the strong fishy flavors. Boil sake if you wish to remove the alcohol content.

SALTED BLACK BEANS

Probably best known as the ingredient used in beef and black bean sauce, these beans are pressed into a block and need to be separated before adding to dishes. If you can't find them then use canned black beans, but don't confuse these with the ready-made black bean sauce.

SCALLION PANCAKES

These are round wheat-flour pancakes that are used for Peking duck. They are found in the freezer section of Asian food stores or are sometimes available where you purchase your duck.

SHAOXING

This is the most renowned Chinese rice wine. It is an amber-colored liquid widely used in braises, soups, and sauces.

SHRIMP PASTE

Also known as gapi, this pungent paste is used to add a rich seafood flavor to Asian dishes. It should be roasted or fried in oil before adding to dishes. Store in an airtight container in the freezer.

SOBA NOODLES

Traditionally these stone-gray colored noodles were made from buckwheat, but these days a lot of brands use a combinaton of buckwheat and wheat. Allow about 3½ oz of dry noodles per person and be careful not to overcook them.

SOY SAUCE

Most people are not aware that there are two types of soy sauce—light and dark. Light soy sauce is used in stir-fries, marinades, and dressings, while dark is used in braises and broths.

STAR ANISE

This star-shaped spice is an integral flavoring in Chinese cooking. It is widely used in bouillon, soups, and braises, and is an essential ingredient in five-spice powder.

SUSHI RICE

This is a short-grain rice used for making sushi as it has a higher starch content, which means it sticks together once cooked. Rinse thoroughly under cold running water before using.

SWEET CHILI SAUCE

This is used as a condiment for fried chicken in Thailand. Sweet chili sauce will vary in intensity and sweetness depending on the brand—try several to find the one you prefer. It is also great in dressings and marinades, and can be thinned with a little water if it is too thick.

TAMARIND

This comes in two forms: a solid block that contains both the pulp and seeds and the concentrate or paste. It needs to be prepared before use: the pulp is broken apart and then covered in boiling water and left to soften. The pulp and seeds are then strained off to leave a sour orange-colored liquid. Tamarind is widely used in Thai cooking to add a pleasing sourness to soups and curries.

THAI BASIL (HORAPA)

The purple-tinged stem and finer, more pointed, leaves are the easiest way to differentiate Thai basil from Greek basil. Thai basil has a much stronger anise flavor than its Mediterranean cousin.

TOFU

Also known as beancurd, tofu comes in a variety of textures: silken, which is mainly used in desserts; silken firm, which is suitable for soups; and firm, which is best for stir-fries and curries. You can also purchase deep-fried tofu, which is delicious added to soups, stir-fries, and curries where it acts like a sponge to soak up the flavor of the sauce.

UDON NOODLES

These are Japanese wheat noodles that are available pre-cooked or dry in food stores. Udon noodles are thick, almost worm-like, and can be used in soups, stir-fries, and salads.

VIETNAMESE MINT

Also known as laksa leaf, this leaf is widely used in Vietnamese cooking—as the common name would imply. Its elongated pointed leaf has a strong spicy mint flavor. If you can't find it use spearmint instead.

WAKAME

This is a type of dry seaweed and is much valued for its flavor and texture. It is widely used in soups (namely miso) and salads, where it marries well with vinegared dressings.

WASABI

Also known as Japanese horseradish, this is sold either in a tube as a paste or in a powder form that needs to be mixed with water to form a paste. Its heat will clear the sinuses, so use sparingly if you don't like hot spicy stuff.

WATER CHESTNUTS

Sold in cans, these are widely available in foodstores. Rinse well before using.

WHITE OR SHIRO MISO

A mild sweet miso that is used in soups and is also delicious in dressings.

WHITE GLUTINOUS ("STICKY") RICE

This is mainly eaten in the north of Thailand where it is always served as an accompaniment to Som Tam (green papaya salad). It can be served either as a sweet or savory rice and needs to be soaked in cold water overnight before cooking to soften the grain.

WONTON WRAPPERS

These square or round yellow wrappers are used for wontons and dim sum. They are available in the refrigerated or freezer section of your store or Asian food stores.

YELLOW ROCK SUGAR

Looking more like a crystal than sugar, this amber-colored sugar is used in Chinese broths and braises to add a gloss to the finished dish.

MENUS

JAPANESE

1
Miso soup.. 07
Edamame.. 12
Gyoza 13
California rolls.................................... 14
Sashimi 17

2
Yaki soba 22
Sesame beef salad 25
Pork tonkatsu.................................... 29
Japanese beef curry.......................... 32

3
Spicy fried chicken............................ 33
Chili chicken ramen........................... 34
Teriyaki chicken 43
Yakitori chicken 45

4
Fish with miso 58
Chirashi sushi 61
Temaki sushi 62

5
Agedashi tofu 63
Vegetable tempura 64
Spinach & bean salad........................ 72

6
Lime & ginger tart 80
Green tea panna cotta 83

CHINESE

1
Chicken & corn soup 06
Dim sum 11
Shrimp toast 16

2
Sung choi bau 20
Char sui pork 24

3
Chicken with cashews........................ 42
Peking duck....................................... 46
Marinated chicken wings 47
Crispy spiced duck............................ 48

4
Asian oysters 51
Steamed fish with ginger 55
Scallops & snow peas........................ 56
Fried rice with shrimp 60

5
Chinese vegetable omelet 67
Steamed tofu with ginger.................. 70
Stir-fried mixed vegetables............... 73
Asian greens 74

6
Watermelon & litchi ice 75
Cashew star anise brûlée 79
Sago pudding.................................... 82

VIETNAMESE

1	Pho bo	08	2	Shaking beef	23
	Goi cuon	09		Bun cha	26
	Nems	10		Bo bun	28
3	Vietnamese chicken curry	39	4	Salt & pepper squid	53
	Vietnamese chicken salad	44		Clay pot salmon	57
5	Pickled vegetable salad	69	6	Black sticky rice	77

THAI

1	Tom yum goong	04	2	Larb moo	19
	Tom kai gai	05		Beef in black bean sauce	21
	Fish cakes	15		Masaman beef	30
3	Chicken pad Thai	35	4	Sweet chili squid salad	50
	Duck & pineapple curry	36		Mussels with lemongrass	52
	Chicken green curry	38		Salt & pepper squid	53
	Stir-fried chicken	40		Seafood red curry	54
	Chicken with lemongrass	41			
5	Vegetable green curry	65	6	Black sticky rice	77
	Steamed tofu with ginger	70		Sticky rice	78
				Kaffir lime crème caramel	81

INDONESIAN

1	Chicken satay	18	2	Babi ketjap	27
				Beef rendang	31
3	Nasi goreng	49	4	Seafood noodles	59
5	Satay pumpkin curry	66	6	Deep-fried bananas	76
	Gado gado	68		Black sticky rice	77
	Noodles with vegetables	71			

TABLE OF CONTENTS

1

STARTERS

2

MEAT

3

POULTRY

NOODLE DISHES

COCONUT MILK DISHES

STIR-FRIES

CLASSICS

4

SEAFOOD

QUICK & EASY DISHES

SIMPLE MAIN DISHES

RICE & NOODLE DISHES

SUSHI

5

VEGETABLES

6

DESSERTS

INDEX OF RECIPES

Note: This index is organized by recipe number.

GENERAL INDEX

Note: This index is organized by recipe number.

ACKNOWLEDGMENTS

Writing, photographing, and publishing a cookbook is by no means a one-woman show. I would like to thank the following essential hardworking members of this team for their commitment to this beautiful book. At Marabout, Jennifer Joly for managing the book through its stages and being a pleasure to deal with, and Emmanuel for the original design and the gorgeous color scheme. Catie Ziller, for pulling it together in a heavily pregnant state. Clive Bozzard-Hill, the cleverest crossword doer I've ever met and oh yeah I'd better mention how fantastic he is at photography and arranging ingredients. His stunning wife, Jane Bozzard-Hill, the book's designer, for doing such a great job with the layout of so many photos.

To Zoe and Lucie for the big smiles they brought home from school each day and for letting me take over their playroom with my props. My wonderful group of assistants who helped me in the kitchen: Sarah Delulio, Rob Allison, and Belinda Altenroxel. Also to Byron, Sasha, Caitlin, and Elice for making my stay in their family home an absolute hoot, thanks for reacquainting me with my inner teenager.

My righthand woman, Tracey Gordon, who makes my job an absolute joy, it was so special to be back in the hot seat with you chef, the fastest chopper/cooker in the West. It was lovely to work again with my editor Kathy Steer who has the amazing ability to calm me from the other side of the world with her watchful eye. Annie, my gorgeous girlfriend, for taking care of all my business stuff while I was o'seas, in between buying and selling a house, and saving people's lives.

Oh and one can't let a cookbook pass by without a mention to my beloved Pridey girl; if you don't own a dog you will think I'm a freak, but if you do you will know their friendship is unrivaled. A big thanks to Dave for taking such good care of her while I was in London shooting this book.

And finally, to my cherished friends and family for being the spine that holds me upright. Your love and tireless support is valued more than Macquarie Bank shares.

Author: Jody Vassallo
Photographer: Clive Bozzard-Hill
Art Editor: Jane Bozzard-Hill
Project Editor: Kathy Steer
English adaptation: JMS Books llp
Layout: cbdesign